RESEARCH OPPORTUNITIES
IN AMERICAN CULTURAL HISTORY

RESEARCH OPPORTUNITIES IN AMERICAN CULTURAL HISTORY

edited by

JOHN FRANCIS McDERMOTT

Published by the UNIVERSITY
OF KENTUCKY PRESS

FOREWORD

THIS BOOK has one purpose: to explore research possibilities in a dozen areas of American cultural history with the aim of awakening students of all ages to rich opportunities for profitable studies of the American past and present. Twelve scholars, whose lively concern has been demonstrated by their publications, sat down together for two days to consider selected fields of interest. In the papers here presented they point out some investigations and evaluations that await the enterprising student.

Research Opportunities in American Cultural History is a report for present and prospective workers. It is neither definitive nor final. It is not a complete account of what has been accomplished in the areas considered nor a complete list of all possible projects remaining. No paper in it is a complete survey of the area reported. It develops no thesis. The book is simply a statement of work to be done, a broadcast of suggestions, an indication of the wide range of subjects to be found in these relatively untilled fields of research.

Obviously other areas might have been included. The cultural history of the frontier, the Spanish in America, business enterprise and exploration before 1860, religion and the cultural development of the West, and democracy are topics that readily suggest themselves. This volume has been limited to twelve areas for the sufficient reason that this was a comfortable number to present at a two-day meeting.

No paper pretends to completeness. Each member of the conference was asked to devote thirty minutes to presenting some of the unworked possibilities that he saw in his field. Any worker in the vineyard can quickly add to the suggestions made here. Annotated checklists of graphic artists working in Pittsburgh, Louisville, Cincinnati, St. Louis, and New Orleans in the nineteenth century would be valuable contributions toward the history of art and interest in art in the Mississippi Valley of that time. Editions of the letters of John Vanderlyn and William S. Mount and the papers of Thomas Cole would make available many documents for American art history. Moritz Busch's *Wanderungen zwischen Hudson und Mississippi, 1851 und 1852* (Stuttgart, 1854) and Karl Theodor Griesinger's *Freiheit und Sclaverei unter dem Sternenbanner; oder Land und Leute in Amerika* (Stuttgart, 1862) are two of many accounts by German travelers that ought to be translated and edited.

Such western newspaper editors as Charles Keemle and Alphonso Wetmore could very well be the subjects of full-length studies. The life of the actor-manager and "southwestern" writer Sol Smith deserves attention. No history of the St. Louis Mercantile Library has even been published, though this institution has had a life of one hundred and fourteen years as a subscription library and for forty years in the nineteenth century maintained also the Mercantile Library Hall, a center where lecturers and musicians contributed to the cultural entertainment of the city of St. Louis. The St. Louis *Reveille* of the 1840's is quite as worthy of attention as the much better known New York *Spirit of the Times*. Newspapers everywhere in the nineteenth century were filled with travel accounts which ought, at the least, to be listed. The Indian has been studied by the anthropologist as if he were an artifact, and by the historian as a pawn in frontier expansion; it remains to approach him as a human being. Religion on the frontier has largely been described in church histories and biographies by the pious; the preacher is yet to be considered as a man in a community. The frontier missionary has been lauded as a man devoting himself to good works under trying conditions; but no one has yet made a study of the fitness of the typical missionary for the work he undertook, though there are many documents on which to draw. These are but a few additional subjects that come to my mind—any of my associates could range in like manner.

Each of the participants in the conference has reported his findings in the way that seemed to him best. While editorial conformity in a volume developing a single point of view is a comfort to the reader, it would be pointless to impose a pattern on a group of papers each of which can stand independent of the others. Within the general limitations of the meeting each contributor has said what he wanted to say as he wanted to say it. One result has been some overlapping. We have left these occasional repetitions, for they illustrate how closely the areas are related and how each enriches the others.

This book, then, is not complete or exhaustive or neatly uniform. But it does have a thousand suggestions to make. It will be worthwhile if young scholars—and older ones, too—are brought to awareness of research areas not before considered.

The possibility of a conference to discuss opportunities in less occupied fields of research I talked over with two of my liveliest younger colleagues at Washington University, David Kaser, then Assistant Director for Technical Services at our library, and Ralph E. Morrow, Associate Professor of History. We planned a program and obtained the support of Lilly Endowment, Inc. To our regret Mr. Morrow withdrew from the Conference because he knew he would be away from St. Louis pursuing, as a Guggenheim Fellow, his studies of religion on the frontier. On October 23 and 24, 1959, we met at Washington University as a round-table. All members were present at the four sessions, participating in the discussions that followed the reading of the papers.

We thank Lilly Endowment, Inc. for making possible this meeting and the publication of the papers; Dr. Manning M.

Pattillo, Associate Director of that foundation, for the personal interest he took in the Conference; and Washington University for being its host. All my visiting colleagues, I think, know how much I appreciate their joining in the Conference and how much I value their contributions. I must add a word, too, for the publisher who has borne with me in getting these papers through the press.

Washington University   JOHN FRANCIS MCDERMOTT
February 1, 1961

CONTENTS

THE COLONIAL
PERIOD REEXAMINED

LESTER J. CAPPON

CHARLES and Mary Beard in *The Rise of American Civilization* prefaced their description of provincial America by declaring that, "In reality the heritage, economics, politics, culture, and international filiations of any civilization are so closely woven by fate into one fabric that no human eye can discern the beginning of its warp or woof."[1] If we may equate culture with civilization and thus interpret cultural history broadly, we can put aside sharp distinctions between political and economic viewpoints, conflicts between social and intellectual historians, and get on with such research and writing as contribute toward a more intelligent understanding of American history.

The cultural concept of civilization provides a suitable framework for consideration of contemporary thought about world problems and rival civilizations. However, as we continue to rewrite the history of American culture, much of the research must be specialized, even local, in order to supply the essential ingredients for an authentic synthesis of our civilization. The parochial is often minimized as inconsequential, but this judgment is valid only when local history has been isolated from its broader cultural context.

Several elements inherent in the colonial history of the United States have seriously affected its historiography for good or for ill. Among these are the didactic and patriotic bent of early nineteenth-century historians, the geographical fragmentation of the narrative, conflict between the colonial and the imperial point of view, and the concept of the "transit of civilization." Since the influence of these elements has persisted into our own day, they may serve as a means of recognizing and evaluating current opportunities for research.

Until 1850 American history was colonial history, ending with the War of Independence and the establishment of the national government. The theme was predominantly political and military. As yet there was little American history in the curricula of school and college, and no professional historians. Just as ancient and European history were colored by close association with moral philosophy, so American annals were didactic rather than objective. George Bancroft's *History* sounded a patriotic, nationalistic note that characterized much of the historical writing of his time; Jared Sparks expressed it in his historical editing as well as in his writing; and Benson Lossing found a responsive public through his pictorial presentation of men and events of heroic cast. By the turn of the nineteenth century, the new professional historians, more dispassionate than provocative and less objective than they professed to be, were inclined to underrate the scholarly attainments of Bancroft and his contemporaries, whose works were tinged with patriotic bias.

The culmination of the colonial period in the American Revolution has always posed a serious problem for the scholar seeking the truth about the beginnings of the United States. The story is dramatic as well as controversial; the *dramatis personae* are dynamic and colorful. The historian finds it difficult to exclude his view of events of 1775-76 from his

1 *The Rise of American Civilization* (New York, 1927), I, 124.

evaluation of events of 1765-66, and to assess the revolutionary era in its own terms and objectives. He must guard against identifying "the inevitable" that preordained the climax of independence. He must deal with propaganda without becoming its victim and with the nationalism of his own country without minimizing its federalism. And the framework, whether of revolution or rebellion, somehow modifies the picture within.

Because the events themselves were controversial, successive historians of this challenging period have become involved in controversy. The clash of provincial politics on either side of the Atlantic at times obscured the principles involved, as the hope of revolution overcame the fear of rebellion. Although belief in the "destiny" of the English colonists to become free and independent is no longer tenable, the American historian nevertheless tends to take satisfaction in the successful revolution that produced the American nation. An awareness of both self-interest and "self-evident" truths as motivating forces increases the difficulty of interpretation. The historian must take both into account. Who are the heroes, who the villains, in this complex story of delayed action and conservative revolution?

One of the most provocative recent interpretations of the Revolution is Edmund S. Morgan's volume entitled *The Birth of the Republic*, on the theme that the history of the American Revolution embraces much more than the years of action after Lexington. "It is the history of the Americans' search for principles . . . [that] finally culminated in the adoption of the federal Constitution. It was a noble search, a daring search, and by almost any standards a successful search." Acknowledging the shortcomings of Bancroft, Professor Morgan points out that Bancroft "did address himself to the central question: How did the United States come into being as a nation dedicated to principles of liberty and equality?"[2] This seeming exaltation of principles over mundane issues and personal interests, with an overtone of patriotism, promptly aroused a critic. According to Max Savelle, Professor Morgan has so

[2] *The Birth of the Republic, 1763-1789* (Chicago, 1956), 3, 158-59.

oversimplified the historical problem that his interpretation of the Revolution "raises more questions than it answers." The controversy brings into focus specific subjects for further investigation and reaffirms the assertion that in the rewriting of history an older viewpoint may be revived and refurbished; that what was once authoritative may fall into disrepute and reappear in a new context. If, as Professor Savelle observes, "historians tend to take on the intellectual coloration of the climate of opinion in which they work,"[3] we may expect further demonstration of principles, challenged in our own generation, as motivating forces in history.

This is the issue in the historical controversy over the adoption and ratification of the Constitution which Charles A. Beard first explained in terms of economic interest in *An Economic Interpretation of the Constitution of the United States* (1913), questioning the arguments over political principles that earlier historians had found as sufficient reason for the contest between Federalists and Antifederalists. Both principle and personal interest are among the historian's facts, as recent critics of Beard have shown. That the issues which influenced each politician's vote for or against the Constitution were complex, Forrest McDonald's study of individual cases has proved and, in doing so, has opened the way for further reassessment of this controversial period.[4] Furthermore, as Professor Richard B. Morris has observed, if the adoption of a system of republican federalism constituted a more thoroughgoing break with the political system of the past than severing the tenuous bonds of empire, "the Federalists, not the Antifederalists, were the real radicals of their day."[5]

Because the story of the thirteen colonies is commonly considered synonymous with early American history, it is

[3] *William and Mary Quarterly*, 3d ser., XIV (1957), 608ff; 618.
[4] Forrest McDonald, *We the People: The Economic Origins of the Constitution* (Chicago, 1958); Robert E. Brown, *Charles Beard and the Constitution . . .* (Princeton, 1956).
[5] Richard B. Morris, "The Confederation Period and the American Historian," *William and Mary Quarterly*, 3d ser., XIII (1956), 156.

fragmented geographically by its very nature. Each colony was a separate political entity, perpetuated, with few exceptions, by statehood. The lack of a unifying element in the broader narrative before 1763 has increased the historian's difficulty of dealing with it on a grand scale. Even the inter-colonial wars break down into localized fighting for the most part. State and local pride has encouraged the writing of history circumscribed by political boundaries and indifferent to economic and social forces which are no respecters of state lines. As Virginia or Pennsylvania or Massachusetts made its own separate history, so the historian has found most satisfaction in treating the individual colony, tracing its relations with the mother country and seeking the antecedents of the revolutionary climax, without concern for parallel events in other colonies. A new crop of colony and state histories, broadly conceived, is needed.

When institutional history was in vogue in the late nineteenth century, its most fruitful laboratory was the several English colonies to which Herbert Baxter Adams directed his students. In the monographs of this "school," the Johns Hopkins *Studies* of the 1880's and 1890's, the development of political and social institutions seems unfailingly divorced from the persons through whom these institutions moved and shaped the course of events. The institutionalists were obsessed with the hypothesis of Anglo-Saxon democracy, originating in the forests of Germany, developing through the English constitution, and flowering in the free atmosphere of America. An unpremeditated examination of the sources could not confirm this hypothesis, which was concerned more with forms than with substance.

During these same years, Philip Alexander Bruce and William B. Weeden were shedding new light on Virginia and New England society from abundant local sources. Weeden's reflections of 1890 should evoke assent from present-day historians: "Yet we have not the whole story. Picturesque narration, philosophic speculation, have not exhausted the forces inherent in history. The life of man, his daily action,—closely allied to his thought and to his affections,—must yield up its fact, its daily doing, before we can comprehend the whole action, the whole story of man in his relation to history."[6] The facts, the "daily doing," were in the local records, as Bruce demonstrated with overwhelming evidence, but few historians have had the patience to follow his example. The perennial questions of political rights and their exercise, of public opinion expressed and implied, of the interplay of aristocracy and democracy, require research at the local level. Here, potentially, is history at the source, provided the historian understands the provenance of the records and the character of the people whose thoughts and actions are recorded in them. Here are cultural data on individual persons and on family kinships which are easily lost in the impersonal tabulation and correlation of statistical data. Recent scholars in early American history, with commendable efforts to draw significant conclusions from their research, provide ample evidence of the pitfalls of method as well as the opportunities for creative interpretation in using the voluminous sources of local history.[7]

At the opposite pole is the imperial aspect of colonial history, with which we associate the research and teaching of Charles M. Andrews. Even before 1900 he challenged the institutional approach which Herbert L. Osgood continued to employ during the first quarter of the twentieth century in his comprehensive works.[8] In calling on American historians to view the colonies within the framework and interests of the

[6] William B. Weeden, *The Economic and Social History of New England, 1620-1789* (Boston, 1890), I, iv.

[7] Cf. Bernard Bailyn, *New England Merchants in the Seventeenth Century* (Cambridge, 1955); Robert E. Brown, *Middle Class Democracy and the Revolution in Massachusetts, 1691-1780* (Ithaca, 1955); Jack P. Greene, "Foundations of Political Power in the Virginia House of Burgesses, 1720-1776," *William and Mary Quarterly*, 3d ser., XVI (1959), 485-506, with a note on method and sources; J. R. Pole, "Suffrage and Representation in Massachusetts: a Statistical Note," *WMQ*, XIV (1957), 560-92, and XV (1958), 412-16.

[8] Note the companion papers read in 1898 by Andrews, "American Colonial History, 1690-1750," and by Osgood, "The Study of American Colonial History," Amer. Hist. Assoc., *Annual Report for 1898* (Washington, 1899), 49-60, 63-73.

British Empire, Andrews swept away some of the provincialism of his colleagues. (British provincialism concerning colonial problems of the Empire, a factor of considerable historical importance, has likewise persisted to some degree in British historiography.) The study of imperial policy and administration has shed new light not only on the center of gravity in London but also on events in the several colonies. "I believe," said Andrews in his pioneering address, "that a reasonable attention given to the history of the Canadian and West Indian colonies will help to elucidate phases of our early commercial history and of British colonial methods."[9] While later scholars have substantiated his belief and provided many of the segments for the *magnum opus* which Andrews himself set out to write,[10] the West Indies to a large extent remain an unexploited historical field. Their riches are apparent in the pages of the late Richard Pares's *Yankees and Creoles: the Trade between North America and the West Indies before the American Revolution* (1956).

It is not to be inferred that imperial history can be written entirely from London or that the individualism of the separate colonies, revealed in the sources on either side of the Atlantic, can be disregarded. Fragmentation endured within the "Old Empire"—indeed characterized it—so that continual study of its component parts is both desired and promoted by the very nature of the records. Even the filing system of Secretary William Blathwayt of the Board of Trade suggests, by his geographical arrangement of the records, frequent dealings of the Board with individual colonies on their separate problems rather than a coordinated handling of administrative business common to all of them.[11] These contradictory factors in the Empire both before and after 1763 offer abundant opportunity

[9] Amer. Hist. Assoc., *Annual Report for 1898*, 58.
[10] *The Colonial Period of American History* (New Haven, 1934-38), of which he completed four volumes on the seventeenth and early eighteenth centuries.
[11] Lester J. Cappon, "The Blathwayt Papers of Colonial Williamsburg, Inc.," *William and Mary Quarterly*, 3d ser., IV (1947), 321, 322.

for further research on such diverse matters as federalism, free trade, and loyalty.

Neglect of imperial history in relation to the colonies cannot be explained away by a dearth of source materials. Andrews spoke from firsthand knowledge of the abundance of resources in the Public Record Office and elsewhere in Great Britain. Other historians in the nineteenth century had delved into them and copied small segments, but Andrews, with the backing of J. Franklin Jameson, actually surveyed and inventoried them. His *Guides*[12] to these records have provided the starting point for every scholar in this field during the past half century. They have inspired other documentary projects, local, regional, or imperial in scope, enriching the colonial period as a whole. The current Virginia Colonial Records Project for inventorying and microfilming records in England pertaining to the Old Dominion began in 1955 with a careful reading of Andrews' *Guides* as the most intelligent approach to the voluminous sources.[13]

Another factor in colonial history is the transplanting and flourishing of English culture in America. By the eve of the Revolution this process had been going on for 150 years; but what became American culture and what remained English will always provoke wide differences of interpretation. Developments in the seventeenth century comprised the substance of Edward Eggleston's remarkable book, *The Transit of Civilization from England to America* . . . (1901). Written several years after Frederick J. Turner's essay on "The Significance of the Frontier in American History" (1893), Eggleston's work fell into obscurity soon after his death in 1902. He did not write to contradict Turner's thesis. Eggleston's theme, "the

[12] *Guide to the Materials for American History, to 1783, in the Public Record Office of Great Britain*, 2 vols. (Washington, 1912-14); Andrews and F. G. Davenport, *Guide to the Manuscript Materials for the History of the United States to 1783, in the British Museum* [etc.] (Washington, 1908).

[13] On the nature and early returns of this important project and on its interesting beginning see Julian P. Boyd, "A New Guide to the Indispensable Sources of Virginia History," *William and Mary Quarterly*, 3d ser., XV (1958), 3-13.

history of culture, the real history of men and women," he had stated publicly in 1900.[14] Among the subjects treated in his *Transit of Civilization* were the "mental outfit" of the early colonists, their speech and folklore, their education, and the social and economic conditions of their daily lives.

Although a generation later his book was the inspiration of two essays, "Civilization in Transit" and "Culture in Knapsacks," by Dixon Ryan Fox,[15] Eggleston has only recently been rediscovered for the general reader as well as the scholar in a paperback edition with an introduction by Arthur M. Schlesinger.[16] This comprehensive approach to colonial culture could not match the challenge of the American frontier as the dominant force in American historiography during the first three decades of the present century, for Eggleston was ahead of his time. His was an ambitious work which needs to be redone with the benefit of augmented source materials and the contributions of modern scholarship during the past half century. A similar study of the eighteenth century is needed, broadly conceived and not restricted by any narrow concept of intellectual history. Numerous monographs have contributed piecemeal to our understanding of English and European culture in America, but few historians have been inclined to look eastward across the Atlantic to seek evidence from the local scene in England. As the "climate of opinion" often affects historical writing, so the concept of the Atlantic cultural community came to be better understood in the wake of World War II.[17]

The expansion of research in American history during the first quarter of the twentieth century and the steady increase of courses in this subject in colleges and universities caused the

[14] In his presidential address to the American Historical Association, "The New History," Amer. Hist. Assoc., *Annual Report for 1900* (1901), I, 47.

[15] Fox, *Ideas in Motion* (New York, 1935), 3-76.

[16] Boston, Beacon Press, 1959.

[17] Cf. Louis B. Wright, *The Atlantic Frontier* (New York, 1947); Michael Kraus, *The Atlantic Civilization: Eighteenth Century Origins* (Ithaca, 1949); Gerald Stourzh, *Benjamin Franklin and American Foreign Policy* (Chicago, 1954).

study of the colonial and revolutionary periods to flourish. The younger generation of the new professional historians had been attracted into this field, in part through the interest of their elders who held the nineteenth-century viewpoints reviewed above. Furthermore, this younger generation produced an impressive company of distinguished scholars—Andrews, Jameson, Wertenbaker, Becker, Bolton, Channing, Greene, McLaughlin, and others—who trained a host of graduate students and proliferated research and publication. Jameson, who was also ahead of his time, wrote *The American Revolution Considered as a Social Movement* as early as 1895. When at length he published it in 1926, having found disappointingly little in it to revise, the book was acclaimed as a new work exemplifying the new trend in social history.[18] None of these scholars regarded themselves as writers of "cultural history" but all of them contributed to a clearer understanding of American culture, however their works may be classified.

During the 1930's, however, a decline of interest in colonial history was in process, though it was not readily apparent from the new books published. To be sure, in the 12-volume *History of American Life*, edited by Schlesinger and Fox, the first four volumes were devoted to the colonial and revolutionary periods, comparing favorably with the space allotted in A. B. Hart's *American Nation* series of 1907. Vernon L. Parrington spent the first volume of his *Main Currents of American Thought* on the years 1620-1800 (1927). Andrews completed the fourth volume of his *Colonial Period* in 1938. Lawrence H. Gipson's first three volumes on *The British Empire before the American Revolution* (1936) gave promise of the large-scale work which he is still carrying on. Yet, despite these notable achievements and the scholarly works of Carl Bridenbaugh, Perry Miller, Samuel Eliot Morison, and others, colonial history was going into eclipse in the college curriculum.

The immediacy of a world in continuous crisis magnified

[18] See Frederick B. Tolles, "The American Revolution Considered as a Social Movement: a Re-evaluation," and Elizabeth Donnan's note on the date of Jameson's manuscript, *American Historical Review*, LX (1954-55), 1-12; 496.

historical events of the present century, so that "our times" seemed the most pertinent and rewarding fare for student and teacher. The loss of historical perspective may be considered a symptom of the times. As enrollment in colleges and universities increased, the number of students in courses on early American history declined. Critical problems of prosperity and depression stimulated research in the social sciences to which the historian made his contribution, but this was chiefly from studies in recent history. Early American history seemed hardly germane to the investigations of the economist and the sociologist; and the political scientist, unlike his colleague Charles A. Beard, was not much concerned with historical origins. Recent history, since the historic year 1865, if not later, seemed adequate as a point of reference for recent issues. What challenge, if any, did colonial life and thought offer for the solution of modern problems?

If this question exposed the constriction of the practical American's mind, the reaction has been forthcoming steadily since World War II. The American has felt impelled to search the past for an understanding and justification of his way of life since other nations and peoples do not accept it at face value. Such phrases as American civilization and American heritage are no longer exclusively on the lips of intellectuals. They are commonly seen and heard in our channels of mass communication. "The neglected first half of American history," which was the subject of two professional papers in 1947,[19] has recovered from its doldrums in the realm of teaching as well as in research and publication. The term "cultural history," as suggested at the beginning of this paper, seems to convey best the comprehensive scope of historical study and its cross-fertilization with other disciplines. During the past decade

[19] Carl Bridenbaugh, "The Neglected First Half of American History," *American Historical Review,* LIII (1947-48), 507-16; Lester J. Cappon, "The Need For Renewed Interest in Early Southern History," *Journal of Southern History,* XIV (1948), 108-18. In 1945 the executive secretary of the American Historical Association complained about the dearth of significant articles on American colonial history submitted to the Association's magazine: *American Historical Review,* LI (1945-46), 577.

American civilization programs have provided interdisciplinary study in numerous colleges and universities, with the result that an increasing number of young historians can converse intelligently with anthropologists and psychologists and test their historical research in new terms and considerations.[20] In the *American Quarterly* of the American Studies Association the historian has found a medium for airing hypotheses that may strike fire in the minds of other scholars in the humanities and the social sciences.

While teaching and research in the colonial and Revolutionary period are no longer exceptional in American colleges and universities, some recent developments may be surveyed conveniently through the program of the Institute of Early American History and Culture. Organized in December 1943 with aid from Colonial Williamsburg, Inc., and the College of William and Mary, the Institute stated as its first objective, "To re-awaken a lively interest in the early period of American history." Its second and third objectives reflected further the desire "to recreate a living civilization of the past for the guidance of present-day Americans" and "to encourage and assist writers and scholars in their studies and research."[21]

When the *William and Mary Quarterly* initiated its Third Series, in January 1944, as a magazine of early American history published by the Institute, scholars enjoyed for the first time the advantage of a periodical devoted exclusively to the colonial and early national period (down to ca. 1815). With Richard L. Morton, Douglass Adair, and Lawrence W. Towner as successive editors the *Quarterly* has continued to attract many contributors and provide constructive editorial criticism. The increase in subscribers, individual and institutional, from less than 700 to some 1600 during these seventeen years affords

[20] On the background and inception of American studies programs see Tremaine McDowell, *American Studies* (Minneapolis, 1948), chs. 3-6; and on recent developments, Robert H. Walker, *American Studies in the United States: a Survey of College Programs* (Baton Rouge, 1958), ch. 3.

[21] *The Institute of Early American History and Culture, Williamsburg, Virginia* [Williamsburg, 1946], 5.

convincing evidence of the resurgence of interest in early American history. Even though the *Quarterly* has no monopoly of articles in this field, its annual content may be regarded as a reliable gauge of historical research, discovery, and criticism. An index to Volumes 1-15, published in 1960, enhances the reference value of the magazine.

As one surveys the articles in the seventeen volumes of the Third Series, he finds numerous interpretive essays as well as fresh factual information; but he will look in vain for a clear-cut historical trend in the nature of the material or the viewpoint of the authors. There are essays equally numerous in what may be classified as social, economic, or intellectual history, but those essentially political exceed any of the others by almost two to one. The student of political history is inclined toward research in depth in the local records, in order to correlate persons with their interests and actions. However, a penetrating study of the Stamp Act, of anti-federalism, or of the Kentucky and Virginia Resolutions may be a contribution to social and cultural history, complementary to the political narrative. Occasionally the editor devotes an issue to a special theme—Scotland and America, or the history of science, for example. Essays in historiography have precipitated or reassessed controversies on historical interpretation, sometimes encouraged by the editor through review articles on new books. As an occasional forum for historical issues, the *Quarterly* aids and abets "living history." The book reviews cover the entire field including works in the history of England and the British Empire as they are germane to early America.

The books published by the Institute, edited during the past six years by James Morton Smith, number some thirty volumes. They too illustrate the diversified interests of scholars in this field. The manuscripts published, which are only a small percentage of those submitted, represent the best of the crop within the financial capacity of the annual budget, supplemented handsomely in 1957 by a grant from Lilly Endowment, Inc. Monographs on such varied subjects as the Quaker merchants of Philadelphia, white indentured servitude, Bacon's rebellion, and the bill of rights reflect the modern scholar's wide horizon within his period. Most of the Institute's books may be regarded properly as cultural history; scarcely any of them could be classified exclusively as economic or political or religious history. Documentary volumes likewise diversified in character are found on the Institute's list, such as Jefferson's *Notes on the State of Virginia,* Franklin's *Letters to the Press,* and Dr. Alexander Hamilton's *Itinerarium.*

During the past decade the Institute has sponsored an occasional conference to discuss special areas that ought to be exploited as virgin territory or redeveloped after prolonged neglect. The plan for these conferences includes publication of the essays and bibliographies in a series entitled *Needs and Opportunities for Study.* At the first conference in 1952, Whitfield J. Bell, Jr., surveyed early American science. His essay and bibliography, including selected bibliographies of fifty early American scientists, has become a much cited work,[22] the starting point and initial guide to a variety of research in this burgeoning field. The most recent conference, in October 1959, dealt with early American education. This is a rich subject, unfortunately shunned by historians[23] and sorely misunderstood by educationists by reason of their unhistorical approach and narrow concept of education. The provocative paper on "Education in the Forming of American Society," by Professor Bernard Bailyn, and his bibliographical essay have been published recently in this series.[24] At the conference on Indian-white relations the common ground of history and ethnology became forcefully evident in the essay by William N. Fenton.[25] Conferences on law and on architecture have not

[22] *Early American Science* . . . (Williamsburg, 1955).

[23] The Third Series of the *William and Mary Quarterly,* through 1960, contains only three articles on education.

[24] Bailyn, *Education in the Forming of American Society: Needs and Opportunities for Study* (Chapel Hill, 1960).

[25] William N. Fenton, *American Indian and White Relations to 1830: Needs and Opportunities for Study,* [and] *A Bibliography* by L. H. Butterfield, Wilcomb E. Washburn and William N. Fenton (Chapel Hill, 1957).

achieved published results; but the field of colonial philosophy has yielded to analysis without a conference and its surveyor, Vincent Buranelli, has suggested through his incisive article in the *Quarterly* numerous opportunities for further research.[26]

Several recent historiographical surveys attest to the flourishing condition of early American history. In the New American Nation series, Louis B. Wright's volume on *The Cultural Life of the American Colonies, 1607-1763* (1957) contains a detailed bibliography, chapter by chapter; and his essay on *New Interpretations of American Colonial History: Selected Writings since World War II* (1959), which he prepared for the American Historical Association's Service Center, is especially useful for getting one's bearings on current trends in historiography. A similar pamphlet for the Service Center is Edmund S. Morgan's *The American Revolution: a Review of Changing Interpretations* (1958), concerning the imperial, the social-economic, and the Namierist schools of thought, a survey complementing the author's "The American Revolution: Revisions in Need of Revising" (1957).[27] These essays are knowledgeable guides for the student as he prepares to do his own probing into the records of the Revolution. The student can go a step farther chronologically by considering Richard B. Morris's critique of "The Confederation Period and the American Historian."[28]

Most formidable and comprehensive among recent bibliographies, though it makes no claim to completeness, is Daniel J. Boorstin's in *The Americans: the Colonial Experience* (1958) —nearly fifty pages, double-column, of descriptive and critical references. In the introduction to the bibliographical essay he declares that "with few exceptions, recent scholarship has aimed at clarifying and amplifying details rather than at reinterpreting the sweep of colonial history, much less at discovering the special character of American civilization."

[26] "Colonial Philosophy," *William and Mary Quarterly*, 3d ser., XVI (1959), 343-62.
[27] *William and Mary Quarterly*, 3d ser., XIV (1957), 3-15.
[28] *William and Mary Quarterly*, 3d ser., XIII (1956), 139-56.

While Boorstin's book is really a wide-ranging series of essays in cultural history, not a sustained narrative of the colonial period, nevertheless, it is both thoughtful and bold, impressionistic and realistic, with Boorstin's own distinctive thesis on the components of American culture and their relative influence.

Frederick B. Tolles, leading authority on the Quakers in America, has suggested a number of "new approaches to research in early American history"—in the long neglected period, the half century before 1750; in the biographical field —governors, scientists, religious leaders, etc.; and on the "middling sort" in society, "the plain people who made up the bulk of the colonial population and who are almost voiceless in history."[29] In the complex task of correlation the "grass roots" may provide the most reliable basis.

This is the level too, on which the sources come to light and the best clues to new discoveries turn up. Through local channels of communication the historical societies and research libraries have accumulated their treasures, essentially from local sources. Twenty years ago the Historical Records Survey was overwhelming historians with its inventories of county records throughout the United States. Today the scholars in the great projects for editing the papers of American statesmen are assembling masses of material in photographic copies, much of it from obscure local institutions and from private hands. *The Papers of Benjamin Franklin,* of James Madison, of the Adamses, and other statesmen, as they appear in successive volumes to complement the pioneering *Papers of Thomas Jefferson,* will provide an abundance of cultural resources, especially on the eighteenth and early nineteenth centuries. If anyone doubts the potentialities of this period for research, he needs only to glance at the increasing contributions by historical editors to the original records in published form.

Cross-currents and conflicting viewpoints in the historiography of the colonial and revolutionary periods are indicative

[29] *William and Mary Quarterly,* 3d ser., XII (1955), 456-61.

of new opportunities for research, just as surely as the discovery of new sources provides assurance of valuable additions to the store of factual information. The study of origins and beginnings has always had a special appeal in history. The climax of early American history in the great revolutionary era finds a ready response in successive generations, and our own is no exception. Great issues and high principles pose a serious problem for the historian to evaluate in their proper context.

As early as 1822 Hezekiah Niles compiled and published *The Principles and Acts of the American Revolution.* The Acts provide some of the facts that reveal the development of early American life and culture. If the principles speak for themselves, they do so most candidly through the well tempered historian, untainted by such patriotism as Eggleston branded "a virtue of the half-developed."[30] The concept of cultural history that is all-embracing in scope and content is substantially the "new history" that he was advocating at the beginning of the present century—"the real history of men and women" which the records will reveal through the historian's quest for truth.

[30] Amer. Hist. Assoc., *Annual Report for 1900*, I, 40.

THE FRENCH IN
THE MISSISSIPPI VALLEY

JOHN FRANCIS McDERMOTT

THE HISTORY of France in the Mississippi Valley is brief. Effective entrance into the Valley was made by Jolliet and Marquette in 1673. Ninety years later France withdrew and, except for a few weeks at New Orleans in 1803, never again had an official voice in Valley affairs But in those nine decades the vast territory from the Alleghenies to the Rockies, from Canada to the Gulf, was explored, and the foundations were laid for two great cities and many lesser settlements. France withdrew, but Frenchmen remained. The concern of this chapter, besides noting what has recently been added to the published record of the activities of these French, is to call attention to many more research trails that will help us to know how they lived and what they lived for.

The writing of colonial Louisiana's political and economic history is now in the able hands of Marcel Giraud, Professor of North American Civilization at the Collège de France. With the archives of France at his elbow he will ultimately complete a definitive history. His thoroughness is indicated by his first two volumes which carry the story of settlement from 1698 only to 1717, and by a third volume in progress which will not go beyond the founding of New Orleans. It will be many years before Professor Giraud will reach the close of the Seven Years War, but we shall eventually have a history that will not be likely to need revision.

In urban history we are less fortunate. Much has been written about New Orleans and St. Louis, but there is no reliable and readable account of either city. Books about New Orleans run to "glamour," as shown in Herbert Asbury's *The French Quarter* and Harnett Kane's writings. Most books that pretend to be histories of St. Louis have been pedestrian compilations of fact, not always accurate. Such excellent works on special subjects, however, as James Musick's *St. Louis as a Fortified Town* (St. Louis, 1941) and Charles E. Peterson's *Colonial St. Louis: Building a Creole Capital* (St. Louis, 1949) will be of great value to anyone attempting to produce a general history of this city.[1]

For other towns of the central Mississippi Valley some carefully documented studies exist, especially for Cahokia, the oldest of these settlements (1699), for Kaskaskia, founded in 1703, and for Ste. Genevieve, dating from 1735.[2] Ovid Bell's *Cote sans Dessein* (1930) records the history of a village founded at the mouth of the Osage River about 1808 by Frenchmen from St. Louis and St. Charles. These studies, well

[1] To these I add a recent paper by Professor Marine Leland of Smith College on an eighteenth century businessman of St. Louis and Cahokia: "Joseph-François Perrault, Années de Jeunesse, 1753-1783," a 76-page reprint from *La Revue de l'Université Laval*, XIII (1958-59). For a glimpse of St. Louis today see Professor Isidore Silver's paper on "La Renaissance française à Saint-Louis," *Technique-Art-Science* (June-July, 1959), 15-35.

[2] Charles E. Peterson, "Notes on Old Cahokia," *French American Review*, I (July-September, 1948), 184-225; John Francis McDermott (editor), *Old Cahokia: a Narrative and Documents Illustrating the First Century of its History* (St. Louis, St. Louis Historical Documents Foundation, 1949); Gilbert J. Garraghan, S.J., "New Light on Old Cahokia," *Illinois Catholic Historical Review*, XI (October, 1928), 99-146. Natalia M. Belting, *Kaskaskia under the French Regime* (Urbana, 1948). Francis J. Yealy, S.J., *Sainte Genevieve, the Story of Missouri's Oldest Settlement* (Ste. Genevieve, 1935); Ward Dorrance, *The Survival of French in the Old District of Sainte Genevieve* (Columbia, Mo., 1935); Charles E. Peterson, "Early Ste. Genevieve and its Architecture," *Missouri Historical Review*, XXXV (January, 1941), 207-32.

based on fact, emphasize the need for a broader investigation of the social and cultural history of the French in Illinois and Missouri.

Many documents, it is true, have already been collected and printed to serve the cultural historian. This material has been published by historical societies and in other series as well as in many single and local volumes which offer splendid hunting grounds for the scholar in search of the color of life in colonial Louisiana.[3] But, though many documents are now available in print, there are many more volumes the publication of which would add to our knowledge and understanding of these Mississippi Valley French. Professor Lawrence Kinnaird, in fact, has waiting for a publisher two more volumes of Spanish documents covering the years 1794-1804. Professor A. P. Nasatir has ready a work entitled *Life on the Spanish Mississippi*, a collection of five diaries kept on Spanish gunboats patrolling the river in the 1790's. Professor Gilbert Chinard has in hand an edition of the unpublished memoirs of Dumont de Montigny, a document vastly superior to the work published over Dumont's name in the eighteenth century. The edition of the unpublished letters of Lieutenant Colonel John Wilkins, British commandant of the Illinois Country, 1766-1769, on which Colton Storm has been working, ought to add much to our stock of specific knowledge of Cahokia and Kaskaskia during those years.

There is no source so rich in the details of daily life as the records of estates, property exchanges, marriage contracts, and other personal papers of a public sort. With the list of a man's

[3] *Wisconsin Historical Collections;* Clarence W. Alvord, Clarence E. Carter, and Theodore C. Pease, eds., *Illinois Historical Collections;* Lawrence Kinnaird, *Spain in the Mississippi Valley, 1765-1794* (3 vols., Washington, 1949); Louis Houck, *The Spanish Regime in Missouri* (2 vols., Chicago, 1909); C. E. Carter, ed., *Territorial Papers of the United States* (9 volumes on Illinois, Missouri, Arkansas, and Louisiana). Something of the color of life in St. Louis, for instance, can be seen in a report made July 13, 1779, by Fernando de Leyba, commanding there, to his governor-general at New Orleans: "There have arrived at this post . . . five boats, all loaded with rum, sugar, and coffee, which for these people are the world, the flesh, and the devil." (Kinnaird, I, 346).

household possessions, one can begin to get an impression of his style of living. With a collection of inventories of estates and records of public sales, one can begin to assess the conditions of life in a town. Certainly a publication of the colonial archives of St. Louis and of other early settlements in the Valley would be invaluable.

Private papers of interest are abundant. Tireless search in state archives and the National Archives, in the great historical collections in the Library of Congress, in the Louisiana State Museum, in the Missouri Historical Society, in the Wisconsin Historical Society, in the Clements Library at the University of Michigan, in the archives at Quebec, Montreal, Paris, and Seville will disclose many batches of manuscripts which ought to be published.

Consider these three examples of what awaits the wideawake researcher. In the Gallatin Papers of the New-York Historical Society there are eighty letters written between 1804 and 1836 at Vincennes by Jean Badollet (as well as forty earlier letters). Here certainly is material for a valuable documentary volume —let me emphasize that a man's papers often prove to be a broader and more useful publication than would be a volume on their writer's life. This can be said about the papers of John B. C. Lucas. Although he was not of a stature to justify a book-length study, the very multitude of his letters belonging to the New-York Historical Society and the Missouri Historical Society, written over a period of twenty years in western Pennsylvania and almost forty more years in Missouri, gives a significant place-and-time interest to this material. Special interest centers likewise in the letterbooks of Charles Gratiot, a French-Swiss-born and English-educated merchant who arrived at Cahokia from Canada in 1777 and settled in St. Louis three years later, engaged in the fur trade and attempted to develop a cartel of merchants in St. Louis, Montreal, New York, London, and on the Continent.

I have been speaking of documents closely associated with the French towns. Exploration and the fur trade with the

Indians are always intriguing subjects. Tabeau's *Narrative of Loisel's Expedition to the Upper Missouri* (published by Dr. Annie Heloise Abel in 1939) was a contribution of the first importance to our knowledge of that country before the transfer of Louisiana. A. P. Nasatir's *Before Lewis and Clark: Documents Illustrating the History of the Missouri, 1785-1804* (1952) offered much new material from European archives.

But just as significant narratives are still to be found as have already been found. When Meriwether Lewis was about to start on his westward exploration, Thomas Jefferson gave him a part of a journal kept in 1794-1795 by Jean Baptiste Truteau of St. Louis, then in charge of a trading venture on the upper Missouri River. Eventually this portion was published, as well as a third section of the journal found in the Archive of the Indies at Seville, but a middle section remained lost. In 1806 Dr. S. L. Mitchill published in the *Medical Repository* some passages from a "Description of the Upper Missouri" by Truteau, and a century and a quarter later Dr. Abel found another fragment of this account among the papers of J. N. Nicollet, though this document, too, remained incomplete. The long missing portions of these Truteau papers do still exist, though they are not to be found in Seville, Washington, or St. Louis. Full contemporary copies of the journal and the "Description," amounting to 338 pages, lie in the archives of Laval University, Quebec.[4]

Forty years after Truteau, J. N. Nicollet (a French astronomer and mathematician who came to America in 1832) explored and mapped the upper Missouri and the upper Mississippi in preparation for his noted *Report Intended to Illustrate a Map of the Hydrographic Basin of the Upper Mississippi River* (1843). His unpublished diaries of the 1830's await, in the Library of Congress, an editor who can appreciate Nicollet's observations of the Indians and of life on the frontier.

A history of the French fur companies would make a valuable contribution to our knowledge of the economics of the frontier.

---

[4] Since this paper was written, I have undertaken to edit the Truteau papers.

H. M. Chittenden's *The American Fur Trade of the Far West* is excellent in its broad sweep; Bernard DeVoto's superb *Across the Wide Missouri* is devoted to one decade in the nineteenth century. Neither book is concerned with the early days of the fur trade in the Mississippi Valley. Occasionally a detailed investigation of a strictly limited subject such as Charles Peterson's "Manual Lisa's Warehouse" is published,[5] but most of the present history of the French companies is thin, general, and repetitious. A thorough study of this first frontier business is needed. Again, those who write about the frontier today are prone to present the mountain man as an invention of William Ashley, ignoring the fact that the principal guides on most of the United States government's westward exploring expeditions were Frenchmen. Certainly an account of the French guides would be lively as well as illuminating.

Religion in the French Mississippi Valley in the nineteenth century has been studied by Father Gilbert J. Garraghan, in *The Jesuits of the Middle United States* (three volumes, 1938), by Louise Callan, R. S. C. J., in *The Society of the Sacred Heart in North America* (1937), and more recently and more locally in Mother Callan's life of Madame Duchesne, the founder of that order in America.[6] Father Garraghan's *Saint Ferdinand de Florissant* (1923) and *Catholic Beginnings in Kansas City, Missouri* (1920) combine ecclesiastical and local history. Joseph P. Donnelly, S.J., in 1949 published *The History of the Holy Family Parish, Cahokia, Illinois, 1699-1949*. A new history of the archdiocese of St. Louis is in preparation.[7]

But our knowledge of religious life in French colonial days is limited to the glimpses we can get from a few letters and reports in Louis Houck's *Spanish Regime in Missouri*, Lawrence Kinnaird's *Spain in the Mississippi Valley*, Etienne Gayarré's

---

[5] *Missouri Historical Society Bulletin,* IV (January, 1948), 59-91.

[6] *Philippine Duchesne, Frontier Missionary of the Sacred Heart, 1769-1852* (1957).

[7] A little material concerning the Illinois Country is to be found in the *Jesuit Relations,* published half a century ago. One unexploited source is the *Annales de la Propagation de la Foi,* the volumes of which contain many letters from America.

History of Louisiana, Old Cahokia, and other collections of documents. Yet masses of material lie untouched in the archives at Seville, in the Séminaire at Quebec, and in Paris. Missionary reports in diocesan archives and vital statistics in local churches are worth exploiting. A most interesting study is yet to be made of the state of religion and religious behavior in the French settlements. A luckier hunter than I may come upon the lost manuscript in which Pierre Huet de La Valinière related the "misfortunes and persecutions" he suffered in the Illinois Country in 1786 when he strove to establish his authority over Cahokia and Kaskaskia as vicar-general under the Bishop of Quebec and had to accept defeat from the local priest who served under the Bishop of Baltimore.[8]

Not much literary work can be expected in the early years of any settlement, the population being too thin to sustain writers. But wherever there are people, there are folktales and folksongs. Professor Ward Dorrance collected such bits in Ste. Genevieve and included them in his study of that place. Professor Joseph Médard Carrière published in 1937 his *Tales from the French Folklore of Missouri,* gathered largely in the district of Old Mines near Ste. Genevieve, where French is still spoken. Other collections of French folklore by Cecelia R. Berry, Irene Whitfield, and Corinne L. Saucier will suggest still further work of this sort to occupy the folklore student.[9]

One may even have the fortune to stumble on an unknown poet such as François Regnier of Missouri, a handful of whose poems have been preserved and are thought to be of genuine interest as poetry, not merely as a local oddity. It is not impossible that some researcher may come on the lost satirical verses of the illiterate Louisiana planter Louis Badins, or Badinsse as he preferred to be called—Boileau-like verses, dictated to a secretary, excoriating local officials. The story of

[8] One version of his story, in verse, was published in Albany in July, 1792.
[9] Cecelia R. Berry, *Folk Songs of Old Vincennes* (1946); Irene Whitfield, *Louisiana French Folk Songs* (Baton Rouge, 1939); Corinne L. Saucier, *Traditions de la Paroisse des Avoyelles en Louisiane* (American Folklore Society, 1956).

Badins told by C. C. Robin in his *Travels in North America* is, I think, very likely true.[10]

Newspapers offer chance for study. Edward Larocque Tinker's annotated checklist of French newspapers published in Louisiana,[11] my own paper "Louis Richard Cortambert and the French Newspapers of St. Louis,"[12] and Georges Joyaux's paper on "The French Language Press of the Upper Mississippi Valley," read at a conference at Washington University in 1956, indicate what may be done.

The language itself has attracted attention and will attract more. I have already mentioned Dorrance's study of the French still spoken in Missouri, to which he appended a fifty-page glossary. Professor Carrière and others have recorded dialects, local uses of standard words, and new terms created by the new life of the region.[13] It is not to be thought that any of these has exhausted possibilities of the study of the French language in the Mississippi Valley.

Libraries are an index of culture, but little attention has been given to book ownership by the Mississippi Valley French. A brief article by Roger Philip McCutcheon in 1937 on "Libraries in New Orleans, 1771-1833" stands almost alone for this most French of all our cities, though another article by McCutcheon six months later concerning "Books and Booksellers in New Orleans, 1730-1830" is closely related.[14] What awaits the researcher is indicated by the inventory of the estate of Jean Baptist Prevost of New Orleans, who in 1769 left a library of 150 titles running to twice as many volumes as well

---

[10] John Francis McDermott, "A Lost Poet of Louisiana," *Bibliographical Society of America Papers*, XLVI (Fourth Quarter, 1952), 387-91.

[11] *American Antiquarian Society Papers*, n.s., XLII (1932), 247-370.

[12] *Bibliographical Society of America Papers*, XXXIV (Third Quarter, 1940), 221-53.

[13] Joseph Médard Carrière, "The Creole Dialect of Missouri," *American Speech*, XIV (1939), 109-19; Carrière, "The Phonology of Missouri French," *French Review*, XIV (1941), 410-15, 510-15; William A. Read, *Louisiana-French* (Baton Rouge, 1931); J. K. Ditchy, *Les Acadiens Louisianais et leur Parler* (Institut Français de Washington, 1932); McDermott, *Glossary of Mississippi Valley French, 1673-1850* (St. Louis, 1941).

[14] *Louisiana Historical Quarterly*, XX (January, July, 1937), 152-58, 606-18.

as sixty-nine undescribed brochures; by that of Jacques Chol of Ouachita who in 1809 left a collection of 462 volumes, including a thirty-five volume encyclopedia; and by that of the Marquis Claude Vincent de Ternant of Point Coupée, who in 1842 left 422 volumes.[15]

In the central part of the Mississippi Valley my *Private Libraries in Creole Saint Louis* (Institut Français de Washington, 1938) reported book ownership by the colonial settlers in that town, and in a paper on "Private Libraries in Frontier St. Louis, 1809-1840" I have touched briefly on some later French libraries there.[16] The earliest collection of books in the Illinois Country, a gift to the Cahokia Mission in 1722, has been described by Arthur Maheux in "La Bibliothèque du Missionnaire Davion au dix-huitième Siecle"[17] and in *Old Cahokia*. Aubrey Starke has discussed later collections in the villages of the eastern part of the Illinois Country.[18] The libraries of two late eighteenth century Frenchmen, Father Pierre Gibault and Barthélemi Tardiveau, have been reported in detail.[19] These scattered investigations of book ownership and reading interests suggest how much more may be found in probate records to illuminate the state of literary culture of the French. Clearly a study similar to my *Private Libraries in Creole St. Louis* ought to be made for Vincennes and, if I may stretch the Mississippi Valley a bit, for Detroit. In Louisiana, it is obvious, a great deal remains for the researcher.

Concerning French art and artists active in the Mississippi Valley only a beginning has been made. In 1951 the Detroit Institute of Arts, for the two hundred and fiftieth anniversary of the founding of Detroit, created an impressive exhibition,

[15] *Louisiana Historical Quarterly,* IX (July, 1926), 429-34; *Bibliographical Society of America Papers,* XLVI (1952), 391; Walton R. Patrick and Cecil G. Taylor, "A Louisiana French Plantation Library, 1842," *The French American Review,* I (January-March, 1948), 47-75.

[16] *Bibliographical Society of America Papers,* LI (First Quarter, 1957), 19-37.

[17] *La Canada Française,* XXVII (March, 1940), 650-61.

[18] "Books in the Wilderness," *Illinois State Historical Society Journal,* XXIX (January, 1936), 258-70.

[19] *Mid-America,* XXVII (Oct., 1935), 273-75; *Illinois State Historical Society Journal,* XXIX (April, 1936), 89-91.

the record of which has been preserved in Paul Grigaut's superb catalogue *The French in America, 1520-1880;* a good part of this book is devoted to the French in Louisiana and in the Illinois Country. In 1953 an exhibition held in New Orleans to celebrate the Louisiana Purchase featured the French settlements.[20] In 1956 at a conference on France in the Mississippi Valley held at Washington University, Charles van Ravenswaay read a paper entitled "Creole Arts and Crafts."[21] But not many more articles could be listed with these.

The contributions by individual artists to the record of life in the Mississippi Valley have had little attention. Of those who wandered westward over the Alleghenies pencil in hand the best known is Charles-Alexandre LeSueur. Lengthy accounts of his activities with considerable checklists of his sketches have been published in the United States by Waldo G. Leland and W. R. G. Vail, as well as several shorter articles, but, strangely enough, no book has been devoted to LeSueur and his vivid report of what he saw along the Ohio and the Mississippi in the 1820's.[22] Hardly known at all is the work of Father Nicolas Point, who was associated with De Smet in the Rockies in the 1840's. Point's reminiscences, now awaiting publication,[23] have particular value, for he was an amateur artist and embellished his narrative with a great many on-the-spot sketches of scene and custom among the Indians and of fur trade forts not otherwise of pictorial record. Doubtless there are other sets of sketches to be recovered.

Many works of travel difficult of access are worth translating. Properly annotated, they can make very useful contributions to our knowledge. Among such recent translations are Richebourg McWilliams' rendering of the Penicault narrative (1700) under the title of *Fleur de Lys and Calumet* and Edward

---

[20] Leonard V. Huber, Samuel Wilson, Jr., and Garland F. Taylor, *Louisiana Purchase. An Exhibition Prepared by the Louisiana State Museum in co-operation with the Louisiana Landmarks Society* (New Orleans, 1953).

[21] *Missouri Historical Society Bulletin,* XII (April, 1956), 213-48.

[22] *Mississippi Valley Historical Review,* X (June, 1923), 53-78; *American Antiquarian Society Proceedings,* n.s., XLVIII (April, 1938), 49-155.

[23] Translated and edited by Joseph P. Donnelly, S. J.

D. Seeber's translation of Edouard de Montulé's *Travels in America, 1816-1817*. Louis Leclerc de Milford's *Memoir or Cursory Glance at my Different Travels & My Sojourn in the Creek Nation,* originally issued in 1802, remained an extremely rare and inaccessible book until it was published in translation in the Lakeside Classics in 1956. The letters of Camille Ferri-Pisani, aide-de-camp to Prince Napoleon on his visit to America in 1861, have just been turned into English by Georges J. Joyaux.

It is not difficult to suggest other travel accounts that may well occupy the translator and editor. Baudry des Lozières' *Voyage à la Louisiane* reports his stay in Louisiana in 1794-1798. Théodore Marie Pavie's *Souvenirs Atlantiques* include an account of his travels in the Ohio and Mississippi Valleys about 1830. The Marquis de Lezay-Marnézia's *Lettres Écrites des Rives de l'Ohio* record his philosophizing in the wilderness in 1790 and 1791. Add to these many others: the Baron de Montlezun, *Voyage fait dans les Années 1816-1817 de New-Yorck à la Nouvelle Orleans;* Prudent Forest, *Voyage aux Etats-Unis de l'Amérique en 1831;* Léo Lesquereux, *Lettres Écrites d'Amérique* [1848-1851]; J. Tolmer, *Scènes de l'Amérique du Nord en 1849;* J. P. O. Comettant, *Trois Ans aux Etats-Unis* [1852-1855]; Charles Olliffe, *Scènes Américaines* [*ca.* 1850].

Such citations remind us, too, that there are works in English that demand critical editions: notably, Henry Marie Brackenridge's *Views of Louisiana* and Amos Stoddard's *Sketches of Louisiana,* source books of first importance for the period of the transfer of Louisiana.

It is inevitable that bibliographical studies will overlap. The existence of Frank Monaghan's invaluable *French Travellers in the United States, 1765-1932* (New York, 1933) does not preclude the desirability of another annotated bibliography made for our area.[24] A work that might with little stretch of

[24] Another important bibliographical work is Henry Putney Beers' *The French in North America. A Bibliographical Guide to French Archives, Reproductions, and Research Missions* (Baton Rouge, 1957).

truth be called *Three Centuries of French Travelers in the Mississippi Valley, 1673-1960* could contain, even for the portion of time paralleling Monaghan's, a number of previously unrecorded titles. Two other checklists—always annotated—are quite as much needed: one of travel accounts published in French periodicals, the other of such accounts in French newspapers, for a vast amount of useful material lies buried in these unexplored sources. The latter project can be made "practical" for an American student by limiting it to French newspapers published in the United States, for example, the *Courrier des Etats-Unis.*

In conclusion a miscellany of suggestions might be made. The Champ d'Asile colony in Texas is worth extended study; so, too, is the Icarien experiment at Nauvoo. Fréderic Gaillardet arrived in New Orleans from Europe in 1837 and traveled through the Mississippi Valley before settling down in New York to edit the *Courrier des Etats-Unis* from 1840 to 1848. Louis Xavier Eyma first visited the United States in 1845 and later wrote many books about America. Both warrant sustained investigation. That enormously prolific writer of westerns, Gustave Aimard, surely would make a subject for a book. Edward Larocque Tinker's *Les Écrites de Langue Française en Louisiane aux XIXe Siècle* (1932) will suggest many possibilities.

Let us look, then, into the diaries and letters of the French settlers, let us search the papers of their estates, let us read their newspapers, let us seek out the records of travelers, let us gather sketches of persons, places, and daily affairs. Let us recreate the lives of these people and see the meaning of life for them. Much has been done toward this end—but much more awaits the adventuring scholar.

INDIAN RELATIONS
IN THE UNITED STATES

HOWARD H. PECKHAM

W HATEVER the New World meant to the Old World —a wilderness to be turned into an empire, an escape for the persecuted or the poor, a source of riches, a vast area of new flora and fauna to be explored and examined—whatever its impact, one thing it was not. It was not uninhabited. In all its parts from the frozen Arctic, across temperate zones, through steaming jungles, along incredible mountain ranges, down to the barren extremity of Tierra del Fuego, this tremendous land mass was occupied by a race new to the European and of an unimagined color.

There were probably at least eight to nine million misnamed Indians scattered on the two continents, with almost a million of them in the area of the modern United States. The Indians were divided into numerous groups of varying cultures and hues and they spoke a bewildering variety of languages. Culture was highest among the agricultural Indians of Middle America and lower among the hunting tribes of the United States, the latter being at a late Stone Age level. To the Europeans this new people seemed a long step backward in time, although some tribes lived in the midst of natural resources rich beyond the wildest European dreams of heaven. Small wonder that the Indian often fascinated his discoverers, and even today continues to interest and also to worry Americans.

Molded in a different culture, the Indian exhibited certain characteristics that frightened, puzzled, or even antagonized the European. He was a contradiction to the basic concepts of Europe; he was not settled, literate, or progressive, the accepted hallmarks of civilization. He lived under a loose form of government, or at least under an authority that did not believe in coercion; yet he sometimes tortured his prisoners of war with savage glee. He was so indifferent to wealth that his extreme generosity shamed the white man. The Indian was lazy and was proud of his laziness, seeing no virtue in mere work. In contrast to Europe's stratified society, the red man attached the utmost importance to individuality; yet he simply could not comprehend individual ownership of land so private that it prohibited trespass. Land, like air, belonged to everyone, and when an occupied spot was abandoned others had a right to move in and utilize it. The Indian had a religion that satisfied him, yet was so tolerant that he appeared to be converted to Christianity when he was often only being polite.

Altogether what infuriated the white man was the Indian's indifference to that which was so obvious: the superiority of the white man's civilization. In the Indians the colonists saw themselves as they were ages ago, and concluded that what these primitive red men needed was civilizing—that is, educating and Christianizing. Any notion that the Indian might be deeply attached to his culture or devoted to his primitivism was too absurd to be entertained; yet in trying to civilize the Indians, the colonists almost destroyed them.[1]

Of course it has been difficult to understand the Indian from the white man's frame of reference. The whole ethic of western Christianity and of economic enterprise was irrelevant

[1] This is one of the themes in Roy Harvey Pearce's penetrating *The Savages of America* (Baltimore, 1923).

to the Indian's aims and thoughts. It became easier to regard this primitive being as an upright vertebrate of the forest, a sub-human that must be shot like a wolf or bear because he was both dangerous and immutable. Nevertheless, in the recesses of his conscience the white man knew that this simple reduction did not cover the situation or excuse it. The Indian, like the Negro slave, was indisputably a human being, probably a child of God, and therefore a brother. Christianity required that he be loved and helped; European secular culture demanded that he be reformed or eradicated. The quandary remained.

As long as the Indian stood as a challenge to accepted ideas, an obstacle to national goals, or a menace to settlement, it was all but impossible to view him with detachment. Only since the closing of the frontier and the last Indian battle, both occurring in 1890, has it become possible for the white historian to deliberate about the Indian and view his impact with some disinterestedness. Even so, today's student of history approaches any study of Indian affairs with certain ingrained attitudes. He is presumably glad that his own race did displace the Indians on this continent; he is pleased that the United States extends from coast to coast in a rough rectangle; he is sure that in a clash of two cultures, one much more primitive than the other, the higher was bound to dominate, and any solution of the conflict by maintaining both—that is, an unspoiled wilderness on the edge of an industrial development —was a romantic delusion.

In consequence of all these attitudes, the white scholar cannot sentimentalize over the fate of the Indian. While he often wishes that cruelty and injustice had been avoided on both sides, he would not change the end result, and so he tends to rationalize whatever his forefathers did. He tends to believe that the Indian was not completely an innocent victim of aggressiveness. He responded to white pressures as his savage nature dictated; unfortunately, his reaction involved particularly repugnant barbarities that provoked in whites a retaliatory drive toward extermination. But if we are going to excuse the Indian for his cruelties, we can hardly impose restraints on the frontiersman who found his wife burned at the stake or tortured by mutilation, his child's brains dashed out against a tree, and his cabin burned. The scholar may express pious wishes that somehow our present boundaries had been obtained without discomfiting the Indians; but this is a statement of almost irreconcilable objectives. He cannot suggest how such a goal might have been achieved. On the other hand, treatment of the Indian since 1890 by the victorious white Americans has been more vigorously condemned and just measures more clearly prescribed.

Abstract justice was on the side of the Indian, but the impersonal forces of an expanding white culture could not be stopped by legal considerations. Historians have disputed the irrepressibility of the conflict in 1861, but no one has seriously suggested that a clash was avoidable between whites and Indians. Europeans were as convinced of their civilized virtues —and logically so, given their assumptions—as the Indians were stubborn about their culture. At least, we do not yet know how peaceful penetration and coexistence could have been achieved.

Another primary difficulty in doing research on Indian affairs before the middle of the last century has been noted by scholars. Although the older Indians produced plenty of artifacts, they left no manuscripts, for the very good reason that they could not write. In consequence, the written records about Indians were produced by white men, their rivals, competitors, observers, enemies, and what not. We have descriptions and expositions by French and Spanish explorers, English colonizers and Jesuit priests, British travelers, fur traders, army officers, Moravian missionaries, naturalists, frontiersmen, and local historians. They are hardly disinterested reports; they must always be used with caution and allowances.[2] The purist might assert that there is no source material, that all information reaches us secondhand through the eyes and hands of others. The historian can only try to make the best of an unsatisfactory situation.

It might be assumed that troubles with Indians living north of the Rio Grande in the seventeenth century had been adequately treated by historians. Yet even this is not true. Prof. Douglas E. Leach of Vanderbilt University has published recently a study of King Philip's War, representing the fruits of latest researches.[3] Still, the Maine phase of the war remains to be examined, an investigation which Dr. Leach intends to undertake. But King Philip's War was not the only Indian eruption of that century. On Good Friday of 1622, Virginia Indians under Powhatan's brother killed more than a quarter of the English settlers along the James River, including the only white man who, as far as is known, had tried to civilize rather than proselyte the natives. The general reaction was a long war of revenge and attrition that lasted for decades. This tragic event emphasizes how little is yet known about the Virginia Indians, and especially about the confederation under Powhatan.[4]

Similarly, the Pequot War up in Connecticut in 1637 provokes unanswered questions. Battles and some incidents are known—in fact, they ornament local histories—but the broader causes and effects are not as clear. For instance, the Pequots had had trouble with Dutch traders before ever the English entered the Connecticut River valley. The result of the war was cataclysmic, for the Pequots as a separate tribe ceased to exist. Dr. William N. Fenton of the New York State Museum

[2] A good short list of historical literature along with ethnological contributions and bibliographical aids was compiled by the Institute for Early American History and Culture, Williamsburg, Va., in *American Indian and White Relations to 1830* (Chapel Hill, 1957).

[3] Douglas E. Leach, *Flintlock and Tomahawk* (New York, 1958).

[4] Darrell B. Putnam, "A Militant New World, 1607-1640," unpublished doctoral dissertation, University of Virginia, 1959. Roy G. Pierce of the Archaeological Society of Virginia has collected materials for history of local Indians.

has urged as a neglected topic "the supplanting of the Indian in New England."[5]

As for the Dutch in New York, Governor Kieft's war on the Indians in 1641-45 and the Indian attack on New Amsterdam in 1655 have earned fresh examination but recently, along with an account of the rise of the powerful Iroquois league.[6] One special difficulty is that early chroniclers of the sixteenth and seventeenth centuries described Indian organization in European terms that were only roughly analogous. It was all they could do; obviously they had to use their own current vocabulary. But the terms often carry connotations today that are not justified by the facts. Thus the early observers spoke of feudal "castles" for settlements and of "nations," "kings," "emperors," "ambassadors," "priests," "princesses," and the like, when such precise offices did not exist and certainly were not hereditary. They implied a nonexistent, sophisticated political and social organization. V. W. Kinietz' notable work on *The Indians of the Western Great Lakes* (Ann Arbor, 1940) summarizes French sources at the time of first contact in expressions that are not free from this defect of language. Political theorists seized upon these chronicles as proof of their own hypotheses about the natural goodness of man, the evils of institutions, and the social contract of government. Inevitably the theories hardened into truisms which in turn were applied to the Indians as interpretations of their hazily observed customs.

Here the anthropologists have been of important help, in seeing the Indians in Indian terms and reconstructing the complexities of tribal organization and intertribal relations. Their findings are the chief reason why the early quarrels and dissatisfactions in Indian-white relations of the seventeenth

[5] William N. Fenton, *American Indian and White Relations to 1830* (Chapel Hill, 1957), 27.

[6] Allen W. Trelease, *Indian Affairs in Colonial New York: the Seventeenth Century* (Ithaca, 1960). A contemporary classic is Cadwallader Colden, *The History of the Five Indian Nations Depending on the Province of New-York* (New York, 1727).

century require rewriting by historians. At the same time the
field is not attractive because local historians, especially in New
England, have tramped it down, rendering the topics tiresome,
garbled, and romanticized. There are innumerable articles and
books which the historian must read in order to ignore
them. Unfortunately also, seventeenth-century American history seems to be receding into the dim distance of medieval
studies, where the chief interest is displayed by those intellectual historians who are concerned with ideas such as the
decline of Puritanism.

Indian history in the eighteenth century has enjoyed somewhat better treatment. In North America racial troubles
merged with wars for supremacy between European powers.
Because King William's War, Queen Anne's War, the War of
Jenkins' Ear, King George's War, the French and Indian War,
and the American Revolution have been studied in some detail,
the role of the Indian has become clarified in those years of
organized conflict. The embroilment of the Indians in European
politics made them pawns in rival efforts to extend empires.
The tribes were alternately wooed and warred on, as they were
persuaded to ally themselves with France or Spain or England.
The very looseness of tribal organization played into the hands
of ruthless Europeans, for the latter discovered that tribes
could be divided. For instance, it was sometimes possible for
English agents to find a disgruntled or vain warrior who was
largely unsympathetic to French pretensions. This warrior was
then honored and praised by the English, and received presents
and promised that he would be recognized as chief by his
brother Englishmen. Not unnaturally he and those he could
influence allied themselves with the English against the Fran-
cophile members of the tribe. The old chiefs would lose their
power, and the tribe's allegiance would go to the English. This
little experiment in king-making became a standard maneuver
of the European powers, even though the Indians always lost
in the victory of their new allies.

Because of ancient hostilities, the various Indian tribes never united to resist all white men. Indeed, it is doubtful if any Indian saw his race's plight in such general terms. A Huron chief named Nicolas tried to revolt against the domination of the French in 1747, but this was a local affair and probably he simply saw advantages in trade with far-wandering Englishmen. In 1762 a Delaware prophet in the Ohio Valley began preaching a kind of pan-Indianism: he exhorted his brethren to give up their economic dependence on the whites, return to the use of bow and arrow, and get rid of the foreign menace by refusing to deal with white men. His program was almost a religious movement, and it uncovered a weakness in the Indian: he enjoyed the higher standard of living made possible by white manufactured goods; self-sufficiency at the cost of a lower living standard simply wasn't attractive. The Ottawa chief, Pontiac, altered this doctrine and advocated throwing out the British and reinstituting the friendlier and more generous French. His uprising in 1763 was fundamentally a reactionary revolt, an effort to revive the past. European treaty making, which he could not comprehend, blocked his plan.

Similarly, the Miami chief, Little Turtle, tried to hold back American advance in 1790 and 1791 and maintain the Northwestern tribes in the economic orbit of the British—who had actually signed away the land the Indians lived on in 1783. The old dream was revived in 1810 by the Shawnee Tecumseh, who sought unsuccessfully to unite the tribes. It was too late and the tribes were too short-sighted and self-interested; his hopes were crushed at Tippecanoe in 1811; his allies were defeated in 1813. Incidentally the continuity of this long chain of revolt has never been examined.

I would not leave the impression that Indians in the seventeenth and eighteenth centuries were always on the receiving end of white influence. There was reciprocity, and the colonists learned much about wilderness warfare, hunting, planting, new foods and medicines, comfortable articles of dress, the canoe and snowshoe, the game of lacrosse, and certain verbal expressions. At the same time it must be pretty well conceded that Indian affairs of the latter part of the eighteenth century have been as thoroughly examined as those in any later period.[7]

These futile attempts, not at Indian independence, but at some sort of partnership, were never clearcut. Fundamentally the whites could not conceive of living side by side with a different culture, especially a pagan one. The tragedy of the Indian was that he never comprehended the price of independence: namely, the necessity of supplying himself with goods provided by a superior culture, or of creating a political organization to handle and withstand outside pressures. The prerequisite was education along the path already taken by the white man. All this assumed an adaptability which the Indian never had. His "incorrigible individualism," as Edmund S. Morgan phrases it,[8] left him vulnerable to land seizure, military defeat, and forcible removal. In unity there has always been strength, and the Europeans and Americans knew this elementary axiom. Only an occasional Indian knew it, but he could not achieve it. Piecemeal the Indians were destroyed or pushed to one side.

By the nineteenth century the Indians were simply resisting the tide of settlement as best they could. They were proving themselves such a menace by 1812 in the Old Northwest that much of the sentiment for war against the British was derived from a fierce desire to cut off the moral and material support that the British gave to the Indians. Black Hawk's effort to

[7] Recent studies in this century are John R. Alden, *John Stuart and the Southern Colonial Frontier* (Ann Arbor, 1944); Randolph C. Downes, *Council Fires on the Upper Ohio* (Pittsburgh, 1940); James T. Flexner, *Mohawk Baronet, Sir William Johnson of New York* (New York, 1959); Lawrence Henry Gipson, *The British Empire Before the American Revolution,* vols. v-ix (New York, 1942-56); Wilbur R. Jacobs, *Diplomacy and Indian Gifts* (Stanford, 1950); *The Papers of Sir William Johnson* (Albany, 1921–), 12 vols.; Howard H. Peckham, *Pontiac and the Indian Uprising* (Princeton, 1947); Nicholas B. Wainwright, *George Croghan, Wilderness Diplomat* (Chapel Hill, 1959); Paul A. W. Wallace, *Conrad Weiser, 1696-1760* (Philadelphia, 1945); Anthony F. C. Wallace, *King of the Delawares: Teedyuscung, 1700-1763* (Philadelphia, 1949).

[8] Edmund S. Morgan, *The Mirror of the Indian . . . with an Address* (Providence, 1958).

stem the white surge only resulted in his defeat and the loss of additional land in 1832. In the South the intelligent Cherokees adopted much of the alien culture in order to anchor their homes. Settled in Georgia, they pursued agriculture, learned to write, and in 1827 even organized a government with a written constitution, opened schools, and published a newspaper. They gave every evidence of civilizing themselves. But the state of Georgia, never noted for racial tolerance and influenced by greed for land, could not stand to see an Indian community developing in its midst. A bitter legal fight was begun to oust the Cherokees, but the United States Supreme Court supported the right of the Indians to remain. Georgia, however, was encouraged by President Jackson to ignore the court decision and she forced the Cherokees finally to move across the Mississippi. Here was the answer, said the Indians, to the solution advocated by the missionaries and humanitarians; here was the reward for imitating white culture!

Sporadic Indian resistance to the westward movement of white Americans continued until 1890, but the attacks were short, local, and never a major military problem. The reservation system, which developed rapidly after the Civil War, was a renewed attempt to make farmers out of hunters and to isolate them on paternalistic islands. It suffered from neglect and political corruption, and it prevented assimilation. Yet it eased the national conscience about the "Indian problem" because Uncle Sam was at least doing something. He was treating the Indians as wards and supposedly protecting them.

Out of dissatisfaction with the reservation system came the General Allotment Act of 1887. Indians were to be given lands individually and be extended full civil rights. To safeguard them from being cheated, however, the land titles would be held in trust by the government for twenty-five years. The new policy, which seemed just and humane, soon revealed disastrous flaws. Parcels of 160 acres of reservation land allotted to families were too small to allow anything more than marginal existence; much surplus land was left over which the government sold to whites; the Indians had no capital or credit with which to buy farm machinery; and at the end of the twenty-five-year period improvident Indians sold or leased their farms to whites and lost or diminished their scanty income.[9] An ostensibly humanitarian policy had turned out cruelly, and finally the Indian Reorganization Act of 1934 reversed the trend and returned the emphasis to the twin principles of tribal organization and joint government responsibility. Western politicians, nevertheless, have remained divided about the new policy. A Congressional resolution of 1953 called for an end to "wardship" and betrayed much ignorance, deliberate or innocent, about the benefits of the new procedures.

Admittedly it was difficult to write about contemporary Indians in the late nineteenth century. There were too many pioneer survivors around, men and women who remembered various personal encounters with the red men, friendly and hostile, and fell into reminiscence without restraint. Early local histories and publications of historical societies are full of this stuff, the residue of too many old settlers' picnics. Moreover, we were committed to the idea of civilized progress.[10] History was an account of progress, and this conviction made the Indian appear inferior culturally and morally. His stubborn resistance to civilization encouraged indifference when it did not stir hostility.

As a character in fiction, the Indian was exploited by James Fenimore Cooper, by the authors of fictional captivity stories, and by the sudden crop of western dime novels. The movies continued to picture a stereotype, and television shows have only extended it. As alternate faithful friend or bloodthirsty foe of his superior white brother, he was a confusing literary figure. By the time Indians had ceased to be a menace, they were already enveloped in the haze of legends. Devotion to national destinies robbed us of inquiries that might better have been made. The work of Schoolcraft, L. H. Morgan, Parkman,

[9] See Gordon Macgregor, *Warriors Without Weapons* (Chicago, 1946).
[10] This theme is developed in Pearce, *The Savages of America.*

Brinton, and Mayer stand out above a vast sea of pseudo-scientific speculation and "subliterary" fiction.

Indian history since the Civil War reveals several blank chapters. We need some analytical and detailed accounts of the actual day-to-day operation of Indian reservations. The Indian question in western politics has not been fully explored. It will not be a pretty story, for it contains elements of greed, selfish interest, and corruption. We need histories of particular Indian tribes; the University of Oklahoma Press is receptive to this kind of manuscript and has published several such studies. We lack an examination of the Federal office of Indian affairs, which has been shifted around among Federal departments, and studies of how it has been administered.[11] In this connection, biographies of some of the more prominent Indian commissioners and missionaries would be enlightening. Some have been conscientious and able; others, scheming or indifferent.

Looking back from today only as far as 1790, we can observe a perplexing succession of national policies. Secretary of War Henry Knox in President Washington's first cabinet held some high notions about civilizing the Indians and boldly favored a federal policy of racial intermarriage to be encouraged by pensions. President Jefferson and Secretary of War Henry Dearborn wanted to teach the Indians agriculture so that they would settle down and realize that they did not need vast lands for hunting. By Andrew Jackson's time, the national attitude had largely changed; treatment of the Indian was determined by what was best for the white man and his "manifest destiny." "Removal" was the key word. When the West began to fill up, there was little leftover land into which to push the Indian. Paternalism that would protect him and develop resourcefulness, instead of encouraging dependence, became an elusive goal.

Finally, in this century, Federal policy was reexamined,

[11] *Annual Reports* of the Commissioner of Indian Affairs are available from 1825 to the present.

largely at the demand of private organizations that were ap-
palled by the situation.[12] When the "forgotten man" became a
political slogan, the Indian, too, was remembered. Tribal
councils were reactivated to administer local justice. Schools
were overhauled to raise standards and to teach vocational
skills of the machine age along with a revival of native arts.[13]
Migration from the reservation to urban life has been encouraged.[14] In a rare burst of national self-humiliation, Congress in
1946 permitted the tribes to sue the Federal Government for
having been cheated more than a century ago in land cessions
at trivial prices.[15] I have spotted these highlights simply to
point out that there has been remarkable oscillation in our view
and our evaluation of the Indian.

These changes are challenges in the field of intellectual
history. The initial attitude of the earliest colonizers seemed to
be humanitarian. Was it overcome by covetousness or worn
out by resistance? Or was it superficial kindness, outside the
Calvinistic doctrine of the elect and unregenerate and the
political doctrine of superior and inferior rights? How much
were France and England influenced by Spanish treatment of
the Indian? Did the United States evolve any new attitude
toward primitive people? How did nativism and Darwinism
affect our outlook upon the red man? What were the factors
that awakened conscience in the 1920's? Recent postwar
creation of technical assistance to underdeveloped nations (the
Point 4 Program) calls for the United States to supply money
and know-how; the recipient nation decides how they are to be
applied and what needs to be done. Is this philosophy the

[12] Lewis Meriam and associates, *The Problem of Indian Administration*
(Baltimore, 1928). This investigation by the Brookings Institution condemned
existing policy and laid the groundwork for the Indian Reorganization Act of
1934.

[13] Evelyn C. Adams, *American Indian Education* (New York, 1946)
evaluated the new program.

[14] La Verne Madigan, *The American Indian Relocation Program* (Association
on American Indian Affairs, N.Y., 1956) is a survey of the first four years of
the movement, with recommendations.

[15] The legal status and civil rights of the Indians up to that time are analyzed
in Felix S. Cohen, *Handbook of Federal Indian Law* (Washington, 1945).

proper one with which to approach our Indians?[16] Such questions, and others, open new doors for historical research.

What have the academicians been doing about the Indian? Some hints may be derived from Frederick J. Dockstader's bibliography of master's theses and doctoral dissertations in the United States, Canadian, and Mexican universities from 1890 to 1955 on the American Indian.[17] A total of 3,684 titles are listed. To classify them according to the information in the index is admittedly difficult. Nonetheless, it is apparent that major attention has been devoted to missions and religious studies (357 titles); archaeological sites (327); linguistics and literature (311); acculturation (233); and Indian ceremonies (184). These account for 1,412 of the total, or about two-fifths. By contrast, topics of particular interest to historians are not often tackled. The federal administration of Indian affairs, for instance, has been the subject of only 30 studies; Indian reservations, 89 studies, and they may be incidental background to a subject other than the operation of the reservation itself; treaties, 22 studies; Indian trade, 65; and only 49 are biographical treatments of Indians. It is true that there were 201 references to Indian wars and Indian participation in our wars, and a great many references are found to particular tribes. But how many of these are incidental or brief discussions of certain aspects, and how few may be considered histories of those wars or those tribes are not known. These groupings simply emphasize that in graduate studies dealing with Indians, the lead has been taken by anthropologists and educationists, to say nothing of folklorists and artists. Very clearly the historians are sparsely and weakly represented.

This trend is unfortunate. To be sure, we are learning more about the Indian, socially and psychologically, and we may perhaps develop more satisfactory ways of encouraging assimi-

[16] The analogy is suggested in Harold E. Fey and D'Arcy McNickle, *Indians and Other Americans* (New York, 1959), chapter 19. This book is an able identification of current problems.

[17] Frederick J. Dockstader, *The American Indian in Graduate Studies* (New York, 1957).

lation both on his part and ours. But this area of concern is not historical. It is redundant, but perhaps necessary, to repeat that the historian is concerned with the past, but not primarily with the measurements and statistics in which the social scientist delights; in particular, he is interested in Indian-white relations from Columbus' discovery down to the closing of the frontier. He focuses on the effect of one race on the other and how the ambitions of the one affected the other: the policies, institutions, and customs that developed in consequence of this contact. The blunt fact is that, as far as the historian is concerned, the anthropologists and folklorists seldom ask the right questions. Ethnohistory is a new field, or more accurately a bridge by which the disciplines of history and anthropology may join.[18] They can help us understand, for one thing, that the difference between red race and white is not biological but cultural. The information and methods of the one expert are brought to the attention of the other.

A further deficiency is that the history of Indian-white relations has been too much in the hands not only of amateurs but of enthusiasts: namely, the journalists and antiquarians. Enthusiasm, as we know of early religious revivals, is heavily tinctured with sentimentalism. Part of the training of the professional historian is geared to make him see with a clear and unprejudiced eye, to discipline himself against enthusiasm so as to measure and evaluate with a knowing and calculating reflection. Yet much of the contemporary documentation is secondhand and colored, as we have seen. From the pens of antiquarians or amateurs it is frequently superficial, credulous, or prejudiced. From journalists, it may be sentimentalized, disproportioned, or aimed toward a predetermined goal.

Indian-white relations are not at present a popular field in graduate studies of history departments. In competition for attention, there are other subjects more attractive, richer in source materials, and vocationally more rewarding. The young

[18] *Ethnohistory* is the quarterly publication of the American Indian Ethno-historic Conference.

scholar who wants to devote himself to Indian history may be warned by his department that the outlook for professional distinction and advancement in this field is bleak. This is the curse of scholarly fashions, but a few incisive performances would alter the reaction. This deposit of cultural and human relations has by no means been mined out. There is much to be studied and much to be learned.

Let me conclude by mentioning two favorable omens, aside from the drawing together of ethnologists and historians remarked above. In the matter of the Indian claims now pending, the Department of Justice, which must argue the government's case, has contracted with Indiana University to assemble all relevant documentary information. This source material on tribes and their movements is being copied and deposited at the Indiana University Library and at the National Archives where it will remain for future use by scholars. Further, the climate of the time, with attention directed to problems of racial integration nationally and of colonialism internationally, has aroused more curiosity about our treatment of the Indians past and present. We are reexamining our position and our successive positions. These developments should stimulate our history departments to reconsider Indian affairs as an area of fruitful investigation.

TRAVEL
LITERATURE

THOMAS D. CLARK

ANY WRITINGS in American history would lack color and interest if it were not for the use of travel accounts as sources.[1] These contemporary views contain important personal glimpses of our past. For Europeans the settlement and development of the North American continent was high adventure. Not only did exploration and settlement of this part of the world open an escape valve for European peoples caught in social and economic lags at home; they also brought about in America a transfer and adaptation of old world institutions. A new world of trade was developed, and international rivalries grew on every hand. For the first time imperial powers were brought into serious rivalries and then into conflict in distant places, with a demand upon all of a nation's resources to protect its interests.

For the individual, settlement in North America meant the beginning of a new life. A great abundance of virgin land offered Europeans opportunities to change their economic and social status almost within a single generation. They could now cross the Atlantic and begin life over in an environment beyond the old restrictions which had bound them in countries not yet fully released from feudalism, from religious bondage, and from political interference with individual choice.

In another field, that of science, the opening of North America to settlement by Europeans had special meaning. Botanists, naturalists, geographers, geologists, chemists, and mineralogists had to expand their classifications in the natural world. Knowledge of new plants and plant adaptations to enviromental conditions on this continent helped men to revise contemporary scientific ideas in this field.[2]

Naturalists who concerned themselves with animals, birds, and fish likewise had to rework their material upon visiting this continent. Some of the best travel accounts are those written by scientists in search of fresh information about new world fauna; and their accounts give excellent ideas of the contrasts between European and American natural conditions. For the modern American these accounts not infrequently answer important questions about the prevalence of various kinds of natural life in the early years of settlement here.[3]

Geographers and geologists, too, were faced with strong

[1] There are several helpful bibliographies in this field. One of these unfortunately has never been completed. This is the so-called Buck bibliography of travel compiled under the sponsorship of the American Historical Association, and is now available on microfilm. Of the published works the following are especially pertinent: Frank Monaghan, *French Travellers in the United States, 1765-1932* (New York, 1933); Jane L. Mesick, *The English Traveller in America, 1785-1835* (New York, 1922); E. Merton Coulter, *Travels in the Confederacy: A Bibliography* (Norman, 1947); Thomas D. Clark, ed., *Travels in the Old South: A Bibliography* (Norman, 1956, 1959); Max Berger, *The British Traveller in America, 1836-1860* (New York, 1943).

[2] Pierre François de Xavier, *Journal fait par Ordre du Roi dans l'Amérique Septentrionale* (Paris, 1744); Thomas Glover, *An Account of Virginia* (Oxford, 1676); James Fredricius Gronovius, *Flora Virginica* (2 vols., 1739-1743); Bernard Romans, *A Concise Natural History of East and West Florida* (New York, 1775); Gilbert Imlay, *A Topographical Description of the Western Territory of North America* (London, 1792); C. S. Sargent, ed., "Portions of the Journal of André Michaux," *American Philosophical Society Proceedings* (Philadelphia, 1889), XXVI, 1-145.

[3] Francis Harper, ed., *An Account of East Florida by John Bartram* (London, 1766); and, *Diary of a Journey Through the Carolinas, Georgia, and Florida from July 1, 1765, to April 10, 1766* (Philadelphia, 1791); Miguel Esteban des Courtlitz, *Voyages d'un Naturaliste, et ses Observations faites sur les trois régimes de la Nature* (3 vols., Paris, 1809).

challenges, and were among the first to sense a sharp impact of distance in considering the surface of North America. Imagine the amazement of explorers and scientists when they first encountered the American river system! Englishmen, especially, were improperly oriented to comprehend the great lengths of American streams.[4] All Europeans were impressed mightily by the force with which the water of streams pushed down to the sea. Spaniard and Frenchman alike, whether soldier, priest, or explorer, discovered how intricate was the network of rivers and lakes. Their contemporary accounts tingle with the high adventure involved in these early explorations. The staggering volume of notes kept by Jesuit missionaries and published in the voluminous *Jesuit Relations* provide rich documentation for a major European approach to the continent.[5]

Hardly had settlements been planted along the Atlantic Coast and in the St. Lawrence Valley before travelers made their appearance. In fact, John Smith himself might be considered one of the first English visitors to publish his experiences in a series of books,[6] thus setting a pattern for the travelogues of his fellow Englishmen. From 1607 to the present the volume of English travel material has grown to huge proportions.[7] Once institutional beginnings were made, visitors came to America on almost every ship arriving from England —merchants, government officials, clergymen, and land scouts for prospective settlers. All of these people came on special missions and their views of the new world were likely to be narrowed by their objectives. Merchants, for instance, were alert to prospects for trade, the exploitation of land for agriculture and the development of mineral resources, the forma-

---

[4] Lewis Evans, *Geographical, Historical, Political, Philosophical Essays* (Philadelphia, 1755); Thomas Nairne, *A Letter from South Carolina* (London, 1776).

[5] Reuben Golde Thwaites, ed., *Jesuit Relations and Allied Documents, 1610-1791* (73 vols., Cleveland, 1896-1901).

[6] John Smith, *The Generall Historie* (London, 1632); and *A True Relation* (London, 1608).

[7] See Berger, *The British Traveller;* and Clark, *Travels in the Old South.*

tion of towns, and the location of roads and harbors. Beyond the settlement line, both merchant-trader and missionary saw the Indian and his way of life from tribe to tribe, and many of these travelers gathered information which even yet is significant in the study of Indian life. Government officials came to see at first hand certain problems in the administration of public policies and laws, and compiled a fairly trustworthy account of the deviations from old-world political patterns.[8]

Whatever the mission or business of the traveler, or whatever his national origin, the new world seemed strange to him. Geography was often baffling and the force of nature was all but overwhelming. Already second generation Europeans on this continent were modifying their national characteristics. The powerful new influences of environment in an expanding western world were unlike anything the foreigner had known before. To comprehend the simple fact of distance was difficult for him, and he never really fathomed the emotional and spiritual change which became a continuous factor in American life. In this process of change, Europeans becoming Americans thought of progress simply as the improvement of the conditions of life with each succeeding year and with each new generation. Progress seemed measurable on the highly visible gauge of growing towns, expanding farming communities, increasing roads, newly built mills, churches, and courthouses, along with conquest of Indians and the forces of nature. When a native talked with a traveler, he spoke in terms of great expectations, seldom discussing the realities of the moment since the latter spoke for themselves.[9]

In a more positive way the whole process of colonization, including the larger aspect of human progress and pioneering,

[8] Edmund Burke, *An Account of European Settlements in America* (2 vols., London, 1757); Alexander Cluny, *The American Traveller* (London, 1759); L. McVeagh, ed., *The Journal of Nicholas Creswell, 1774-1777* (New York, 1924).

[9] John Mitchell, *The Present State of Great Britain and North America* (London, 1767); Tyrone Power, *Impressions of America During the Years 1833, 1834, and 1835* (2 vols., London, 1836); Thomas Cooper, *Some Information Respecting America* (London, 1794).

found ready chroniclers in those travelers who made continuous efforts to analyze the processes of change. A genuine travel account obviously had to be written by someone who had traveled somewhere to view the scenes he described, though there were, of course, armchair travelogues of pure fabrication.[10] Too often the foreign traveler came poorly conditioned to accomplish what he promised. He seldom understood what he saw, and in many instances emotionally and intellectually never left home.

One of the greatest shocks suffered by early visitors, especially by the British, was the fact that people only, not environments, were transferred across the Atlantic. This inability to see a rising new civilization in the new American environment marred scores of travel accounts down to 1860.[11] The immigrant came under the influence of American environment the moment he strolled down a gangplank to set foot ashore. On the other hand, the traveler could either accept or reject conditions as he found them. The fact was that many of the English visitors closed their books with the refrain that they were glad to have visited North America, but were really overjoyed to slip back into the civilized atmosphere of their island. At the end of his visit, one traveler wrote: "And now for a detestable voyage (for how can a winter voyage across the North Atlantic be otherwise than detestable?). Sea sickness, storms, and horrors of all kinds: With prospects, however, of speedily enjoying the happiest moment (to a British traveller) of every tour—that on which he touches British soil again."[12]

Before 1787, travel accounts tended to lack the well-centered interest or purpose which they acquired once a unified nation came into existence. A larger number of accounts were written by officials who had business dealings in only a single colony

[10] *Travels in North America* (Dublin, 1822), author unknown; James Shoran, *The Adventures of James Shoran* (Baltimore, 1808).

[11] Thomas Hamilton, *Men and Manners in America* (2 vols., Edinburgh, 1833); Joseph Gurney, *A Journey in North America* (Norwich, 1841); Charles Augustus Murray, *Travels in North America* (2 vols., London, 1839).

[12] J. R. Godley, *Letters from America* (2 vols., London, 1844), II, 243.

—or in only two or three colonies.[13] Consequently their travels and human associations were limited in scope. People who came as missionaries or traveling preachers saw little of life on a broader scale; for example, the Quakers had eyes for little else than the affairs of their own faith. They traveled long distances apparently without seeing much of the country, or failed to leave descriptions if they did see much of it.[14] Yet there were some travelers who braved the rigors of bad roads, nerve-racking stage journeys, and sea travel to get a good view of the colonial system.[15]

Before 1776 few travelers looked upon colonial America as anything other than an adventure in colonialism in which British influence early became a predominant factor. While the view of colonial people emerging from these early books is often badly fragmented, there are occasionally penetrating observations. Occasionally an official or crown view comes into focus.[16] Strange to say this material lacks any appreciable sense of the rising friction between the colonies and the crown. Occasionally a Tory spoke his piece about the agitations which led to the Revolution; but generally the scholar will search a

[13] Samuel Wilson, *An Account of the Province of Carolina in America* (London, 1862); Frank H. Norton, ed., *Exiles in Virginia*, by Thomas Gilpin (Philadelphia, 1848); Hugh Finlay, *Journal Kept by Hugh Finlay* (Brooklyn, 1867).

[14] John Churchman, *An Account of the Gospel Labours* (Philadelphia, 1749); Thomas Wilson, *A Brief Journal of the Life, Travels, and Labours of Love in the Works of the Ministry* (Dublin, 1728).

[15] James Adair, *The History of the American Indians* (London, 1775); Johann David Schoepf, *Reise durch einige mittlern and sudlichen Vereinigten Staaten* (Erlangen, 1788); Pierre F. X. de Charlevoix, *Journal d'un Voyage dans l'Amérique Septentrionale* (Paris, 1744); George Fox, *A Journal or Historical Account of the Life, Travels, Sufferings, Christian Experiences and Labours of Love . . .* (London, 1766); John Bartram, *An Account of East Florida and His Diary* (London, 1766); François, Marquis de Barbé-Marbois, *Our Revolutionary Forefathers* (New York, 1929); Jonathan Carver, *The New Universal Traveller* (London, 1779); François Jean, Marquis de Chastellux, *Travels in North America* (Dublin, 1787).

[16] James Glen, *A Description of South Carolina* (London, 1761); Frank H. Norton, ed., *Journal Kept by Hugh Finlay* (Brooklyn, 1867); H. E. Baird, ed., *The Journal of Lieut. William Feltman* (Philadelphia, 1853); William Strachey, *The Historie of Travaile into Virginia Britannia*, ed. R. H. Major (London, 1849).

large volume of books to locate a few nuggets of fact on this phase of American history. In the Revolution itself a few travelers were able to give a view of the transitions which were taking place in politics, in the process of the war, and in the general framework of society itself.

After 1787 the travel literature about America became more exciting. Now there was a new focal point of interest in the great experiment in federalism. The propaganda for independence had emphasized freedom and democracy so much that travelers came to examine the applications of the doctrine expressed in the Declaration of Independence and the new state constitutions. Some, of course, came to see the federal system fail in its application of the idealism of Jefferson and Franklin. One thing, however, stands out in this period and in the years to follow: George Washington made enormous personal appeal to Englishmen and Europeans who came near Philadelphia or Mount Vernon. He was more than a military leader who had defeated the British. He was the physical embodiment of eighteenth-century democratic idealism.[17]

The states in the Confederation stood in a new economic relationship not only to each other, but to the old world. On a smaller scale the individual states represented a pattern of functioning federalism which was to characterize the formation of the nation. They were the seedbed of the new American system of government. For visitors from abroad few or no previous experiments in government involved so many innovations or local adaptations. This was the first time that a potentially major nation had begun its existence wedded to the idea of applied democracy. This in itself was enough to draw visitors interested in political ideas to observe the young nation in its formative years. They came both to see firsthand what was happening and to suggest ideas which they believed worthy of trial. Travelers have never been timid in making suggestions,

[17] Ferdinand Marie Bayard, *Voyage dans l'interieur des Etats-Unis* (Paris, 1791); Albert Matthews Smith, *Journal of William Loughton Smith, 1790-1791* (New York, 1955), 75-79.

and in the late eighteenth century any number of people had dreams about how a free people could best govern themselves. Philadelphia in time swarmed with politically inspired visitors, and at times the broad porch at Mount Vernon must have been a veritable political forum.[18]

Democracy in action, however, had a far greater field of action than Philadelphia and Washington. It was reflected in the habits, customs, and social maturity of the people; after 1776 the people were in the process of becoming Americans. Some of the population apparently had matured in a manner that accorded with the best European and British standards. The great mass, however, were regarded as crude, uncultured, brash, and repulsive. Washington had set a good personal example of dignity and decorum, but some of his immediate successors in the presidency hardly gave their ages a comparable tone, despite the highly cultivated nature of Jefferson himself. In the travelers' eyes, the federal period was a time of repulsive personal habits, of raw pioneering, and social confusion.[19] Large numbers of travelers were unable to penetrate the surface to comphrehend the dynamics of the new nation and its society. Something approaching panic characterized the efforts of travelers to fathom American life. Even presidents of the United States were drawn from their labors by inquisitive travelers who came to discuss political theories, philosophical ideas, books, practical politics, federalism, commerce, and farming.

Between 1800 and 1860 travelers circulated constantly on the "grand tour," which was from New York to Boston and back, to Philadelphia, Baltimore, and Washington, then south

[18] Talbott Hamlin, *Benjamin Henry Latrobe* (New York, 1955), 75-79.
[19] Una Pope Gregory, ed., *The Aristocratic Journey; being the Outspoken Letters of Mrs. Basil Hall Written During Fourteen Months Sojourn in America, 1827-1828* (New York, 1931); Thomas Hamilton, *Men and Manners in America* (2 vols., Edinburgh, 1831); Basil Hall, *Travels in North America* (3 vols., London, 1929); Charles W. Janson, *The Stranger in America* (London, 1807); Frances Trollope, *Domestic Manners of the Americans* (2 vols., London, 1832). A different point of view is expressed in Adam Hodgson, *Letters from North America* (2 vols., London, 1824).

to Richmond, Charleston, Mobile, New Orleans, and up the
Mississippi to Louisville, Cincinnati, and Pittsburgh. Often
this tour went to the Ohio and Mississippi valleys on the first
leg. Because of this general routing much of the travel literature during the first half of the nineteenth century followed
a set geographical pattern.[20]

Following the organization of the Federal Government, three
subjects became basic themes: government and politics, slavery,
and the rise of towns and cities as trade centers. A great
majority of the travelers, whether or not they were able to
understand the complexities of slavery as an institution, came
with already fixed opinions about it. Because of rising criticism
at home, British visitors especially were vigorous in their
writings about the institution. A considerable number of
travelers made comparisons between conditions in the free
and the slave states. To all foreign travelers, the existence of
slavery in a country so heavily committed to a democratic
political philosophy was the great contradiction of life.[21]

American methods of farming were as interesting to foreign
travelers as was slavery. They saw here a traditional mode of
farm life adapted to a large landed area. The isolated life of
the American farmer, separated by considerable distance from
his neighbors, was in sharp contrast to farm organization in
Europe and England. Land usage, methods of cultivation,
types of field crops, and management of farm animals also
offered material for much comment. Wastefulness of resources
often caught the eyes of frugal Europeans who came from
areas where farming was carried on in a very conservative
manner.

[20] The route followed by Christian Schultze, *An Inland Voyage* (2 vols.,
New York, 1810) outlines the western half of the "Grand Tour;" Alexander
Mackay's *Western World* (2 vols., London, 1849) represents the other half.

[21] James Stirling, *Letters from the Slave States* (London, 1857); Frances
Anne Kemble, *Journal of a Residence on a Georgia Plantation in 1838-1839*
(London, 1863); Charles Lyell, *A Second Visit to the United States* (New
York, 1849); Frederick Law Olmsted, *A Journey in the Seaboard Slave States*
(New York, 1856); Frederika Bremer, *The Homes of the New World* (New
York, 1853).

Travelers' descriptions of American farming are to be trusted only so far as elements of truth become discernible by comparison with modern farm life in America. The average traveler was too inexperienced in this aspect of American life to make trustworthy comments. In one respect the traveler's view was trustworthy in discussing farming. He was able to make some astute observations on the differences between farm life in the South, on the spreading frontier, and in the middle states and the East. The frontier farm taxed his imagination. He was quick to see the slovenliness of the southern cotton farm, and the thriftiness and good order of the Yankee farm strongly appealed to him.[22]

For the most part travelers were city or townspeople who scarcely knew what they were seeing, to say nothing of understanding precisely the life of country people. The crudeness of manner and dress, the dirt of the country taverns, the constant chewing of tobacco, the rancid smells, the coarse language, and the whining accents of rural Americans caused many foreigners to look upon the natives they saw along the way as little more than savages.[23] Again, travelers perceived a sharp contrast between the people of the eastern part of the United States and those of the South and West.[24]

American institutions attracted hundreds of visitors. Prisons were major attractions, and literally scores of visitors knocked on the gate of the Philadelphia Prison asking to be allowed to

[22] George Flower, *History of the English Settlement in Edwards County, Illinois* (Chicago, 1882); Richard Flower, *Letters from Lexington and Illinois* (London, 1819); Elias Pym Fordham, *Personal Narrative of Travel in Virginia, Maryland, Pennsylvania, Kentucky* (Cleveland, 1906); and, William Cobbett, *A Year's Residence in the United States of America* (1819).

[23] Andrew Evans, trans., *A Trip to the Prairies and in the Interior of North America, 1837-1838,* by Count Arese (New York, 1934), 35-39, 46-48; Charles Augustus Murray, *Travels,* I, 120-129, 148-149; Louis Xavier Eyma, *La Vie aux États-Unis* (Paris, 1876).

[24] Edward A. Kendall, *Travels Through the Northern Parts of the United States in the Years 1807 and 1808* (3 vols., London, 1809); Charles Lyell, *A Second Visit to the United States of North America* (2 vols., London, 1849); Karl Theodore Greissinger, *Freiheit unter dem Sternenbanner* (Stuttgart, 1862).

inspect it. Jailhouses and state prisons elsewhere were also visited eagerly by foreigners. Schools, colleges and universities, insane asylums, and hospitals attracted travelers to their doors. As many travelers were reformers at heart, they wished to compare the management of corrective institutions in America with those at home.[25]

Every traveler visited some cities and towns. Here the great horde of observers felt more at home, and their detailed descriptions of urban life are to be accepted as being more worthwhile than those of the countryside. The American city, however, was often puzzling to foreigners. It lacked the neat order and careful planning of many cities abroad. The influence of architects and artists was lacking. Buildings were constructed in highly individualistic and often tasteless designs. Few massive memorials and monuments stood in the streets, and few memorial parks and circles gave use and beauty to public thoroughfares. Private houses were constructed in small single-family units, and people lived away from their businesses. The most striking feature of the American city, however, was that the aspect of permanence was lacking. Everywhere streets were being dug up or rerouted, and buildings were being pulled down to give way to larger and more efficient structures.[26] In the post-Civil War years visitors were frequently startled by seeing houses being moved down the streets from one site to another. Nothing stayed in place. No monument was sacred, no public building was safe from the wrecker. Even church houses had to give way to change and progress.[27]

Four years of civil war brought a crop of travelers to the United States. American democracy was on trial. Political

[25] Franklin D. Scott, tr. and ed., *Baron Klinhowström's America, 1818-1820* (Evanston, 1952), 100-101; James Silk Buckingham, *America, Historical and Descriptive* (3 vols., London, 1841), I, 50-61.

[26] Adam Hodgson, *Letters*, I, 151-181; S. Reynold Hole, *A Little Tour in America* (London, 1859), 249; Felix Klein, *America of Tomorrow* (Chicago, 1917), 67.

[27] William E. Adams, *Our American Cousins* (London, 1883), 208.

observers, diplomats, newspaper men, authors, and opportunists all recorded their impressions of the country in travail.[28] Once the country was actually involved in armed conflict, military men from many countries visited the headquarters of commanding generals, the battle lines, and the war departments of the two sides to view what was happening. Both Grant and Lee knew what it meant to have foreign observers as guests in their military councils. Because of the tense drama of war, and the specialized preparation of many of the travelers, the Civil War descriptions are among the best of the travel books about the United States.[29]

Once smoke cleared from the battlefields, visitors came to see the country in a process of reconstruction, and to gain impressions of the great age of both geographical and industrial expansion. The postwar visitors could move more rapidly about the country than did their predecessors. The route of the grand tour was for the most part relocated.[30] There were, of course, many who visited the South to see what had happened to the region during four years of war, and to find meaning in the end of slavery and the rise of the free Negro.[31] After the slaves were freed, the emancipated Negro in American society became a favorite topic, and traveler comment on this subject becomes important—not because the visitors brought with him experience enough to render wise judgment on the

[28] Samuel Phillips Day, *Down South: or, An Englishman's Experiences at the Seat of the American War* (London, 1862); W. C. Carson, *Two Months in the Confederate States* (London, 1863); David P. Conygham, *Sherman's March Through the South* (London, 1865); James William Massie, *America: the Origin of Her Present Conflict* (London, 1864).

[29] Anthony Trollope, *North America* (Philadelphia, 1863); Catherine Cooper Hopley, *Life in the South* (London, 1863); Charles Frédéric Girard, *Les États Confedérés d'Amérique Visités en 1863* (Paris, 1864); Edward Dicey, *Six Months in the Federal States* (London, 1863).

[30] George Augustus Sala, *America Revisited* (2 vols., London, 1893); Mary Allen Olney, *The New Virginians* (Edinburgh, 1880); Margaret McVeagh, tr., *American Reconstruction, 1865-1870,* by Georges Eugene Benjamin Clemenceau (Toronto, 1928); William Hepworth Dixon, *New America* (London, 1867).

[31] One of the best of these works is Sir George Rose, *The Great Country: or, Impressions of America* (London, 1868); William Saunders, *Through the Light Continent* (London, 1879).

subject, but because in his naive way he gave some insight into race relations.[32]

More travelers, however, followed the feverish trek westward. They wanted to visit the Great Plains, Utah and the Mormons, California and the Pacific Coast. The West had become a pulsating new land with all the thrills of the frontier plus many of the travel conveniences of the modern age. Railroads hauled most of the foreign visitors over the grand tour to California and back. Many travelers strayed as far south as Texas and as far north as Seattle.[33] The great objectives, however, were the new cities. Chicago, raw, bustling, growing, fighting its way upward to become an American commercial nerve center, characterized the new materialistic America.[34] St. Louis seems to have attracted almost half the population of Germany as visitors, to say nothing of the travelers of other nationalities. So did Denver, Salt Lake City, San Francisco, Dallas, Houston, New Orleans, and Charleston.

From 1850 to 1890, hundreds of travelers were able to capture the spirit of expansion which was thrusting the population westward.[35] Often they were unable to identify the force they described, but lack of permanence on both the rural scene and in rising urban America disturbed them.

The earliest travelers to visit Anglo-America commented on education, or lack of it. Hundreds of visitors concerned them-

[32] Sidney Andrews, *The South Since the War* (Boston, 1866); Elizabeth Hyde Botume, *First Days Amongst the Contrabands* (Boston, 1893); Sir George Campbell, *White and Black; the Outcome of a Visit to the United States* (London, 1879); Sir Charles Wentworth Dilke, *Greater Britain* (Philadelphia, 1869).

[33] A. Maurice Low, *America at Home* (London, 1905); Anthony Jenkinson, *America Came My Way* (London, 1956); André Siegfried, *America Comes of Age*, trans. H. H. and Doris Hemming (New York, 1927); T. S. Hudson, *A Scamper Through America* (London, 1882); H. Hussey Vivian, *Notes of a Tour in America* (London, 1878).

[34] S. Reynold Hole, *Little Tour*, 249; Felix Klein, *America of Tomorrow* (Chicago, 1911), 67; Frederick E. Smith, *American Visit* (London, 1918).

[35] A. D. Richardson, *Beyond the Mississippi* (Hartford, 1867); James Bryce, *The American Commonwealth* (2 vols., New York, 1896); Robert Athearn, *Westward the Briton* (New York, 1953); Alexander Lambert de Sainte-Croix, *De Paris à San Francisco* (Paris, 1885).

selves with the process of American education. They visited schools and colleges, inspected libraries, museums, and scientific laboratories. They sometimes examined textbooks, visited professors, quizzed students, and discussed the purposes for which private schools were established. In the great body of travel accounts there is developed a reasonably good profile of American education. Almost no foreigners understood precisely the objectives of the American educators and schools; few understood the public school movement. As universal education became a more prominent fact in American cultural life, it proved more confusing to foreign visitors. Even in the twentieth century foreigners still find our academic procedures puzzling. This has been especially true of those literary lights who invaded this country from 1890 to 1945,[36] and who went from a one-night lecture stand to the next, confronted by eager American undergraduates who seemed both immature and blasé as compared with the serious young men of Oxford and Cambridge, or of Berlin, Vienna, and the Sorbonne. The American female in search of learning hardly had a counterpart anywhere else in the world.

As America grew more prosperous and anxious to acquire culture, the railway cars were crowded with British literary men, government officials, and titled aristocrats hastening from one lecture engagement to another.[37] En route they became experts on American culture, materialism, and restlessness. Everywhere there were commercial traveling men peddling goods and stories. Hotel lobbies were crowded with people attending conventions. These Americans away from home got drunk, gorged themselves on food, cut juvenile capers, and even did a good amount of philandering. Sophisticated visitors looked upon this restless horde as leading a new form of

[36] Hector Bolitho, *Haywire: An American Travel Diary* (New York, 1939); Low, *America at Home;* Siegfried, *America Comes of Age;* Roberts, *And So to America;* Sisley Huddleston, *What's Right with America* (Philadelphia, 1930).

[37] L. P. Jacks, *My American Friends* (London, 1933); Cecil Roberts, *And So to America* (New York, 1947); Huddleston, *What's Right with America.*

animalistic existence in which the almighty dollar became a main objective of human life.[38]

Generally it may be said that the postwar accounts lack some of the rich human interest materials of those written in the earlier years of the nineteenth century; yet they are more numerous, cover a wider geographical scope, and often are more precise in their descriptions. On the other hand, the rising metropolitan press recorded its raw and uninhibited story of this late nineteenth century growth and social chaos. What the traveler did not actually see at first hand, he extracted from the news columns.[39] The postwar newspaperman struck the travelers as being a blood descendant of the brash frontiersman who had stood about steamboat landings making prophecies and bragging about his accomplishments. Too few travelers saw Americans in their homes and about the routine of daily affairs to paint an extensive picture of domestic life, though travelers like Frederika Bremer and Fanny Kemble lingered long enough to take a second look into home life.

Though the family and the home as institutions received little comment, American food was a favorite topic. Most travelers appreciated the fact that Americans had an abundance of food. For many it was strange food, and the mode of its preparation was even stranger. The eighteenth-century Englishman was no better equipped to appreciate American food and methods of cooking than are twentieth-century Englishmen. For many of them, eating in hotels, restaurants, and roadside taverns, the food was greasy, poorly cooked, badly served, and made unappetizing by its very abundance. Eating habits were in keeping with the poor preparation of food. The American was in a hurry so he gulped down his meals, using his hands instead of knives and forks, and drinking cold water in such amounts as to frighten Englishmen who had fixed

[38] Low, *America at Home;* Hudson, *A Scamper;* Bolitho, *Haywire.*
[39] Francis J. Grund, *The Americans in their Moral, Social and Political Relations* (2 vols., Boston, 1837), 121-23; Kendall, *Travels,* I, 146-148; Hudson, *A Scamper,* 214-15; Price Collier, *America and Americans from a French Point of View* (New York, 1897), 267-85; Anthony Jenkinson, *America,* 220-28.

notions about the functions of the digestive tract. The tooth-pick was nearly always in evidence. Conversation was lacking during meals, and there were no leisurely meals where eating was made an art instead of a physical necessity. Yet as the cities grew, as hotels developed dining rooms, and as quality restaurants came into existence, travelers' attitudes softened toward American foods and dining habits.

If the American at home was slighted in the travel accounts, certainly the traveling American was brought into full focus. Whether native sons and daughters were viewed above swaying stage coaches, on steamboats, or on railway cars, they attracted attention. They appeared as crowds milling in streets, as smaller groups riding stage coaches, or strolling about steam-boat decks; but wherever they appeared, they presented a collective national face. Out of the generous descriptions of the people in crowds, certain national characteristics can be fairly well classified. The American on the move was restless, he was garrulous, inquisitive, and often a braggart. In casual conversation with foreigners he was quick to express confidence in his expanding country. This American aboard a Pullman car presented the same general appearance as his forefathers aboard steamboats, but with the major difference that he was smug about his accomplishments. Speculators, traders, peddlers, preachers, adventurers, family men, dandies, ras-cals, gamblers, greenhorns, pompous stuffed shirts, political hacks, pious missionaries, innocent maidens, Yankees, Irishmen, Frenchmen, German immigrants, rugged laboring men, row-dies, Negroes, and actors, all of these were described by travelers. They left a grand composite picture of the people.

For the modern historian travel accounts are peep-holes to the past. No other historical source supplies precisely the type of intimate firsthand information that is to be found in this body of literature. Not even newspapers supply the same kind of contemporary information, nor write with the same per-spective and wide scope of coverage. Diarists may present intimate personal views of life in a given age, but their information is highly circumscribed and for the most part static in nature. Seldom does this personal material have the grand sweep of a major travelogue or the freshness and detachment characteristic of a foreign observer.

Historians, literary people, and social scientists of every sort have used travel accounts with considerable freedom, sometimes without exercising the necessary precautions to insure the validity of their interpretations. Hundreds of these books are of inferior quality, and some of them are marvelous only in the fact that they were ever published.

At the outset several questions must be asked of travel accounts. What was the nationality of the traveler? Where did he come from? What reasons did he give for traveling? What were his special economic, social, or political interests? If he were a Quaker visiting Quaker communities it is likely that he saw or thought little about anything but Quakers. Both George Fox and John Woolman traveled through interesting country, but they recorded almost none of their non-religious experiences.[40] Preachers and religious workers often made miserable observers. They were so preoccupied with congregations, sermons, and theological arguments that they had no time for anything else, and where they did record their views and experiences they marred them by overemphasizing their special interests.

The same thing can be said about many commercial and political travelers. The commercial visitors have left good accounts of economic life, but often they expended their energies in making comparisons with old-world economic conditions. Politicians, especially the British, spent much time in Washington sitting in the Congressional galleries trying to make sense out of American political procedures. Many of them viewed Washington as both the political and social hub of the nation. They went to official receptions and parties,

---

[40] *The Journal and Essays of John Woolman,* ed. Amelia Mott Gummere (London, 1922); Power, *Impressions;* Bolitho, *Haywire;* George Fox, *A Journal or Historical Account of the Life, Travels, Sufferings* (London, 1694).

tramped the streets viewing the city's architecture, and gained an impression of American character from the conduct or misconduct of members of Congress.[41]

Perhaps no other people attach quite the same importance to travel accounts as do the Americans. Almost from the beginning of foreign visitation to the earliest settlements in the new world, Americans were self-conscious and anxious to make impressions upon visitors. Never have we been hesitant about revealing to travelers the most intimate parts of the great American dream. Our aspiration and our national pride have all been stripped naked before our visitors.

In a broader sense the foreign visitor has fired our ego, has taunted us into refining our habits, has revealed weaknesses in our political and social institutions, has criticised our arts, and our letters and press, our cities, and our public manners. Alexis de Tocqueville and Lord James Bryce analyzed our institutions in two of the ablest critical appraisals we have. These semi-travel accounts are quoted wherever estimates of American social and political history are discussed.[42] Only within the past decade have historians discovered the highly prophetic passage in de Tocqueville regarding the rising American and Russian powers.

A phenomenal volume of descriptive literature had been written about the United States, and the end is not in sight. No doubt as many travelogues are produced today as at the height of their nineteenth-century popularity. Since the end of World War II thousands of travelers have visited this country, and no one can know how many travelogues will be published by exchange scholars, students, statesmen, and political observers. Every time a foreign delegation arrives on a university campus, or visits a city and a factory, one reckons the end results in terms of future books. How many packs of letters to folks back home will turn into published accounts is

[41] Mackay, *Western World;* Power, *Impressions;* Bolitho, *Haywire;* William H. Charlton, *Four Months in North America* (Hexam, England, 1873).

[42] Alexis de Tocqueville, *Democracy in America* (2 vols., New York, 1939); Bryce, *American Commonwealth.*

an open question. For example, a young Austrian arrived in Chicago in 1950 to begin his American stay. Three days later he wrote a long letter to a local editor explaining the failure of American race relations. Professor P. E. Dustoor of the University of Allahabad came to the United States as a delegate to a Rotary convention. His 325-page book, *American Days* (Calcutta, 1952) described what he saw and experienced, and it doubtless convinced many of his countrymen that life in the United States was as he saw it. The significance of such accounts lies not so much in what they reveal to us about ourselves, as in the images they create in the minds of other people about life in America.

As for ourselves, visitors long ago became a fixed part of our national life. So long as they keep coming, we can tell ourselves that we are an exciting and alert people. In later years we have even subsidized visitors to come to the United States. We have used the freedom with which they are able to travel here as an effective weapon in the great struggle between the democratic and communist worlds.

From John Smith to Nikita Khrushchev visitors from abroad have viewed the American scene. Mr. Khrushchev, to be sure, has published no account of his recent visit, but this was done for him by the world's newsmen, photographers, radio commentators, and editorial writers. These detailed public reports on important state visitors comprise a new and rather important type of travel literature which reflects the political interrelationships of nations.

This symposium is intended to be suggestive rather than definitive. Travel literature is, of course, well known to scholars in many fields, and it is used in the preparation of hundreds of books and articles. There is lacking, however, sufficient bibliographical assistance both in locating and appraising this great mass of materials. The important project of listing travel books and articles in a great national bibliography under the patronage of the American Historical Association failed of fruition. One or two national group bibliographies, and one regional bibliography cover a considerable body of materials.

Before scholars can be made fully aware of travel accounts as historic sources it will be necessary to ferret out the hundreds of other brief travelogues which were published in periodicals and newspapers. This will be an enormous undertaking, but it will be richly rewarding. This is also true of unpublished letters which lie untouched in foreign and American household trunks and libraries. So long as new and unexploited travel materials exist, scholars must regard the writing of much American social and cultural history as largely an open-end undertaking.

Specifically, travel accounts offer unlimited opportunities for scholarly research and writing in the field of social history. Historians have yet to present a broad study of the structure of American society. Before this can be done acceptably, more research is necessary in the mountainous volume of travel literature and description. This material adds the third dimension of outside observation. In turn no full judgment can be made of this material without understanding something of the structure of American society itself. Research in social history of necessity involves a resort to contemporary and personal sources.

Elements of our history such as population movement, location of immigrant groups, and the orientation of foreigners to American conditions are vividly reflected in visitors' observations. Public health and the occurrence of violence, of economic failures, and of social frustrations are discussed in travel books and articles. Few sources reveal so clearly the elementary impulses which led to entries of claims for large blocks of public lands and town sites; they drilled prospective settlers in the ways of reaching and acquiring them. In this day of soaring book prices, and the growing scarcity of this type of original material for sale, the scholarly hand could be set to far less productive tasks than editing and reproducing series of carefully selected travel accounts.

THE SAGA
OF THE IMMIGRANT

THEODORE C. BLEGEN

HE NEWER emphasis upon the history of immigration has been forwarded in recent years by increasing concern about cultural and social forces in the national life, coupled with the emergence of trained scholars who found immigration, without the coloring of filiopietistic bias, an inviting and challenging research domain. They felt that the frontier hypothesis of Turner by no means explained the diversity in American customs and attitudes or revealed the full complexion of American culture, and that a new approach was needed.

The wide-ranging saga of the immigrant opened fresh avenues to the understanding of American history, though the newer school of scholars did not erect any single theory or hypothesis. American civilization is too complex to be comprehended through any one all-embracing interpretation or thesis. Scholars were interested in the interplay of Old World backgrounds of thought and practice with the New World environment, and were aware of processes of "acculturation," although they did not make much use, if any, of that impressive word. When, in 1922, Arthur M. Schlesinger published his *New*

Viewpoints in American History, the first essay in his book included a sympathetic interpretation of "The Influence of Immigration on American History," and his opinion that "the two grand themes of American history" were "the influence of immigration upon American life and institutions, and the influence of the American environment, especially the frontier in the early days and the industrial integration of more recent times, upon the ever-changing composite population."[1]

We are never far away from Turner, however, in our thinking about large forces in American history. He did not explore American immigration history carefully and critically; but early in his career—even before he wrote his famous frontier essay —he asserted that the story of the peopling of America had not yet been written. "We do not understand ourselves," he said, and in viewing the immigrants, he looked beyond their "bone and sinew" and realized that they "brought with them deeply inrooted customs and ideas." He believed that the American destiny was interwoven with theirs, and later he wrote, "We shall not understand the contemporary United States without studying immigration historically." It is fair to say that he viewed immigration, not merely as a recurring problem, as did many of his generation, but as a constant and significant factor in American history. In his major exposition of frontier influences, he paid very little attention to the impact of millions of immigrants, but in some degree he foreshadowed the newer school.[2]

We cannot write the history of American immigration without drawing upon diverse kinds of materials. The most baffling problem for the historian is to realize that immigrants are

[1] *New Viewpoints in American History* (New York, 1922), 2. See also Professor Schlesinger's revision of this essay under the title "The Role of the Immigrant" in his *Paths to the Present* (New York, 1949), 51-76, with an excellent bibliographical note, 286-89.

[2] Turner's essays on "The Significance of History" and "Problems in American History" are in *The Early Writings of Frederick Jackson Turner* (Madison, 1938), 63-64, 82. See also his articles in the *Chicago Record-Herald,* August 28, September 4, 11, 25, and October 16, 1901. Much of his later basic thinking is recorded in his "Middle Western Pioneer Democracy," *Minnesota History Bulletin,* III (August, 1920), 393-414.

people, not nicely tabulated statistics, and that to understand people calls for the use of sources as varied and far-reaching as their interests and activities, their minds and emotions, their work and ambitions, their frustrations and happiness, their very lives.

Among the many sources that offer research possibilities for the study of immigration are the ballads and songs produced in great numbers and many languages by and about immigrants from the European countries to the United States. An illustration may be found in "Oleana," with its satirical stanzas hailing Ole Bull's immigrant colony in Pennsylvania and describing America as the land where fantastic dreams came true—as indeed they did, though not precisely in the terms of this Scandinavian ballad from the 1850's. Across the waters from Norway, according to the song:

> They give you land for nothing in jolly Oleana,
> And grain comes leaping from the ground in floods
>   of golden manna.
>
> And ale as strong and sweet as the best you've ever
>   tasted,
> It's running in the foamy creek, where most of it is
>   wasted.
>
> And little roasted piggies, with manners quite demure,
>   Sir,
> They ask you, Will you have some ham? And then
>   you say, Why, sure, Sir.[3]

Every country had such ballads, their gay irony not quite masking the essential truth of their claims. A Swedish song from the same period closes each of its many stanzas with the refrain:

[3] For the full verse translation of "Oleana," see Theodore C. Blegen, *Land of Their Choice: The Immigrants Write Home* (Minneapolis, 1955), 282-83. The original text, with a prose translation and the music, appears in Blegen and Martin B. Ruud, *Norwegian Emigrant Songs and Ballads* (Minneapolis, 1936), 187-98.

> Isn't that impossible?
> Ah, but it is wonderful!
> Pity that America
> Is so far away!

Pity, indeed, for this was the picture:

> Trees that strike their roots in earth
> Sweet they are as sugar,
> Country full of maidens—
> Lovely dolls they are, Sir.
>
> Chicks and ducks come raining down,
> Steaming hot and tender,
> Fly upon your table,
> Knives and forks in place, Sir.[4]

Such ballads remind us that the immigrant was a human being, and they also illustrate the fact that the sources for interpreting immigration are varied and are connected with literature, folklore, language, and music, as well as with sociology, economics, and politics. In my exploration of immigration sources, I have found the texts—in many instances the music—of more than a hundred emigrant ballads. I have noted with interest the use that Dr. Kolehmainen has made of Finnish songs and ballads in his emigration studies.[5] More recently Arnold Schrier, writing about *Ireland and the American Emigration,* quotes Irish ballads, including the unhappy one of "Noreen Bawn," who sailed off

> To that place where the Missouri
> With the Mississippi flows.

She returned to Ireland, died, and her weeping mother sang

[4] Theodore C. Blegen, *Grass Roots History* (Minneapolis, 1947), 43-44.
[5] See John I. Kolehmainen and George W. Hill, *Haven in the Woods* (Madison, 1951), and Blegen and Ruud, *Norwegian Emigrant Songs and Ballads.*

'Twas the shame of emigration
Laid you low, my Noreen Bawn.[6]

The emigrant ballads touch not only emigrant dreams of
what America might be, but also homeland conditions, the
reasons for emigration, farewells, the Atlantic voyage, and
varied experiences—good and bad—in the New World. It is
time to launch a cooperative hunt for such ballads in many
languages, to translate them into English, to give them appropriate interpretation, and thus to make them available to
students of American history and culture. The fruits of such
a hunt would provide an addition to our folk literature and
perhaps contribute new insight into the thoughts and emotions
that accompanied the migrations which statisticians present
in tables.

One of the weaknesses of filiopietists, alongside their parading of immigrant claims and their emphasis on heroes and
"contributions," was their failure to search out rigorously the
basic sources for the stories they wanted to tell. What they did
is not without value, but their documentation was as inade-
quate as their methods were uncritical. We cannot deal
responsibly with research opportunities in this field unless we
give thought to primary sources and their availability, and
here we need to be reminded that the history of American
immigration is trans-Atlantic, and indeed international in a
broad sense. Sources, in abundant variety, are to be found in
the Old World as well as in the New. Our subject is in no
sense parochial.

Sources in the Old World need to be ferreted out not only
because they are vital to the understanding of emigrant backgrounds and the impact of America on the Old World, but also
because the story of immigration is richly recorded in contemporary letters that went back by the millions to home

[6] Schrier, *Ireland and the American Emigration 1850-1900* (Minneapolis,
1958), 99. In a chapter entitled "The Invisible Result: Cant and Custom," Mr.
Schrier presents the texts of several other Irish emigrant ballads.

communities. Have they been preserved? Can they be found and used? To a surprising degree, the answer is Yes. Bundles of "America letters" are preserved by countless families in various European countries; and in some of those countries, including the Scandinavian, nineteenth-century newspapers printed vast numbers of letters reporting experiences, bright or dismal, in America—all this as part of spirited national debates on the merits of emigration, thus reflecting a pervasive European curiosity about the United States. The discovery of America did not end with Columbus.

Historical treasures have been garnered from such sources. A few years ago, in *Land of Their Choice*,[7] I brought together English translations of representative "America letters" found in Norway—letters having a nineteenth-century sweep from New York to California and from Minnesota to Texas. I did this partly because the story they unfolded was interesting, original, and significant, and in part because I wanted to forward a movement for gathering up and making available to students of American history similar letters from all countries in the Old World. With some of my friends, I have dreamed of a twenty-volume work covering a century of migration and bringing together in English translations "America letters" and diaries as preserved in all the countries of Europe. Perhaps the plan was overambitious. It has not been realized, but much has been done and more will be done. A scholar in Wales has made a collection of Welsh immigrant letters that promises substance for many community and state studies in the future. American efforts, too, have encouraged the collecting of such sources in some of the European countries, especially the Scandinavian. An illustration is afforded by Norway, where a federation of local historical societies has for more than thirty years gathered up "America letters" for deposit in a national center for original historical sources.

[7] In addition to *Land of Their Choice*, see The *"America Letters"* (Oslo, 1928), and "Early 'America Letters'," in Theodore C. Blegen, *Norwegian Migration to America, 1825-1860* (Northfield, Minn., 1931), 196-213.

The letters are a common people's diary, its interest heightened because the contemporary recorders were personally experiencing a change of worlds. They describe the physical migration in a thousand details; but as the reader follows the records through decades, he begins to realize, as Professor Mulder has observed, that "the immigrant crossed more than an ocean and a continent." His "traveling was . . . across the sprung longitudes of the mind / And the blood's latitudes."[8] We must not forget that the "America letter" was read by many people. The letters mirror the image of America formed in the minds of great numbers of Europeans. That image "was changing, and reflected kaleidoscopic scenes through decades when America was moving westward," and its quality is derived not only from "the external events recorded, but also from the changes mirrored in the thoughts and reactions of immigrants" through the years.[9] The letters are also of value for their detailed documentation of events and changes in the succession of frontiers where they originated.

It would be a mistake to leave the impression that immigrant letters constitute the only source that opens inviting opportunities for research. My own interest in the field began with a book of travel and description, Rynning's *True Account of America,* which I translated and edited many years ago.[10] I soon found myself deep in travel literature, archives, the immigrant press, memoirs, newspapers abroad, and a host of other sources, not omitting statistics. Much can be done with the historical use of European travel and observation in

[8] See William Mulder, "Through Immigrant Eyes; Utah History at the Grass Roots," in *Utah Historical Quarterly* (January, 1954), 41; and the same author's *Homeward to Zion: The Mormon Migration from Scandinavia* (Minneapolis, 1957), xi. The phrase is quoted by Mr. Mulder from John Ciardi.

[9] Blegen, "The Immigrant Image of America," in *Land of Their Choice,* 8-14 and (for the phrases quoted), xi-xii. One of the best articles on the interest and value of "America letters" is George M. Stephenson, "When America Was the Land of Canaan," *Minnesota History,* X (September, 1929), 237-60.

[10] Minneapolis, 1926. The original was published in Christiania, Norway, in 1838.

America, as Nevins, Commager, Handlin, and others have demonstrated in their anthologies. The immigrant press has been only lightly tapped for serious historical studies, in part because of linguistic obstacles, in part because newspaper files are widely scattered and often inaccessible. A national microfilm project is needed here, and its outlines were sketched at a conference held recently in Cleveland at the call of Carl Wittke, a leader in immigration research and writing. The immigrant newspaper press is a storehouse of source material for research in virtually all aspects of immigrant life in America in the nineteenth and twentieth centuries.

There has been much advance in immigration studies since Marcus Lee Hansen in 1927 described "Immigration as a Field for Historical Research."[11] That essay, in text and notes, still points the way to many special studies worth doing, especially in the area of community and group life, where, as the author believed, "the leaven in the lump can be detected." Hansen is rich in ideas and suggestions, but I shall not itemize them here since his article is well known and readily accessible. It would be enlightening, however, as a clue to research potentialities, to glance at work done since Hansen wrote his essay. Such a glance will serve as a guide not only to things done but also to comparable and related studies that might be attempted.

Hansen's career was cut off all too early, but in 1940 his three major books were published—*The Atlantic Migration, The Mingling of the Canadian and American Peoples,* and a volume of essays entitled *The Immigrant in American History.* Taken together they document his basic ideas, the sweep of his interest, his critical research, and his prescription, by scholarly example, of therapy for the filiopietists.

Dr. George Malcolm Stephenson, drawing upon Swedish sources, illustrated and interpreted "America letters" and also explored with acumen the religious aspects of immigration with reference to the Swedish migrants. Scholars interested in

[11] *Am. Hist. R.*, XXXII (April, 1927), 500-18.

Norwegian migration have detailed European backgrounds and the American environmental experience in a long shelf of books, many of them documentary, which offer not a few suggestions of things that might be done for other immigrant groups. Dr. Carlton C. Qualey has written an illuminating study along the lines of flow and distribution[12]—a kind of research that seemed highly important to Hansen. Some of the many-faceted aspects of immigration research are illustrated in path-breaking works by Einar Haugen, Kenneth Bjork, Michael Kraus, and Henry A. Pochmann. They illuminate the linguistic interpretation of immigrant transition, the migration of professionally trained men, eighteenth-century parallels in the transit of culture, and the impact of German thought and literature upon America.[13]

In *West of the Great Divide* (1958), Dr. Bjork has given fresh illustrations of the historical value of the immigrant press as source material; and William Mulder has found and used abundant Mormon sources. Charlotte Erickson, exploring a quarter century from 1860, has advanced knowledge of immigrant labor recruitment by American industry. New socio-historical approaches and substantial contributions in studies of immigrant urban experience have been made by Oscar Handlin in *Boston's Immigrants* (1941) and by Robert Ernst in *Immigrant Life in New York City, 1825-1863* (1949). Henry S. Lucas has uncovered rich treasures in immigrant memoirs and related sources for the story of the Netherlanders in America. For the Irish there are new scholarly works that are a far cry indeed from earlier writings in this field. Dr. Wittke and Father Barry have deepened our understanding of the German migration; Kolehmainen and others have used varied sources for the history of the Finns in America; and the Jewish

---

[12] *Norwegian Settlement in the United States* (Northfield, Minn., 1938).

[13] Haugen, *The Norwegian Language in America: A Study in Bilingual Behavior* (2 vols., Philadelphia, 1953); Bjork, *Saga in Steel and Concrete* (Northfield, Minn., 1947); Kraus, *The Atlantic Civilization* (Ithaca, 1949); Pochmann, *German Culture in America: Philosophical and Literary Influences, 1600-1900* (Madison, 1957).

tercentenary has elicited a number of interesting and valuable studies.[14]

Merle Curti's *The Making of an American Community* (1959), though not primarily an immigration study, is a full-length exploration of the processes of acculturation in a single community. And this reminds me of a somewhat unusual essay on segregation and assimilation in a small Wisconsin community by the sociologist, Peter A. Munch, which illustrates nicely the wedding of sociological and historical methods.[15] Nativism is a recurring phenomenon in American life and politics; interest in this field is not of recent origin, but several notable contributions have appeared lately, especially by R. A. Billington, John Higham, and Robert A. Divine; and Barbara Solomon has done brilliant interpretive work in her historical analysis of "ancestors and immigrants" in a New England setting.[16] A significant trend, definitely influenced by the newer school of immigration historians in the United States, is the increasing attention now being devoted to the impact of migration upon the home countries. A half dozen books have

[14] In addition to the titles specially mentioned in this paragraph, *see* Erickson, *American Industry and the European Immigrant, 1860-1885* (Cambridge, Mass., 1957); Lucas, *Netherlanders in America: Dutch Immigration to the United States and Canada* (Ann Arbor, 1955), and *Dutch Immigrant Memoirs and Related Writings* (2 vols., Assen, Netherlands, 1955); Carl Wittke, *The Irish in America* (Baton Rouge, 1956); James P. Shannon, *Catholic Colonization on the Western Frontier* (New Haven, 1957); Sister M. Justille McDonald, *History of the Irish in Wisconsin* (1954); Wittke, *Refugees of Revolution: The German Forty-eighters in America* (Philadelphia, 1952) and *The German Language Press in America* (Lexington, Ky., 1957); Colman J. Barry, *The Catholic Church and German Americans* (Milwaukee, 1953); Handlin, *Adventure in Freedom: Three Hundred Years of Jewish Life in America* (New York, 1954); Rufus Learsi, *The Jews in America* (Cleveland, 1954); and W. Gunther Plaut, *The Jews in Minnesota* (New York, 1959). Since the preparation of this paper an excellent book on *Finnish Immigrants in America, 1880-1920*, by A. William Hoglund, has appeared (Madison, 1960).

[15] "Segregation and Assimilation of Norwegian Settlements in Wisconsin," in *Norwegian-American Studies and Records*, XVIII (Northfield, Minn., 1954), 102-40.

[16] Billington, *The Protestant Crusade, 1800-1860* (New York, 1938); Higham, *Strangers in the Land* (New Brunswick, N.J., 1955); Divine, *American Immigration Policy, 1924-1952* (New Haven, 1957); Solomon, *Ancestors and Immigrants: A Changing New England Tradition* (Cambridge, Mass., 1956).

appeared within recent years relating to English, Irish, and Scandinavian backgrounds, and the distinguished Norwegian historian, Halvdan Koht, has written a wide-ranging interpretation of *The American Spirit in Europe* (1949), with "a comprehensive view of the effect of American activities, struggles, and efforts upon European life and progress."[17]

I mention these writers and books, not with any thought of offering an inclusive bibliography, but as instances of significant work. The time may come when there will be a master synthesis of the history of American immigration, but, like the great American novel, this may prove an unrealized and unrealizable dream. Dr. Stephenson's *History of American Immigration* (1926), though a pioneering effort, was limited largely to immigration "as a factor in American political development." *We Who Built America* (1939) by Dr. Wittke brought together in a large frame the results of hundreds of studies up to that time; and in 1951 Handlin presented an eloquent interpretation in *The Uprooted*. We have still not achieved the great synthesis, however. Louis Adamic made some effort in this direction, but his approach was a reversion to the indignant and defensive mood and to the parading of claims. His *A Nation of Nations* (1945) is described by the historian of immigrant historiography as "virtually a glossary of the errors committed by the amateur investigators of immigrant history."[18]

[17] W. S. Shepperson, *British Emigration to North America* (Minneapolis, 1957); R. T. Berthoff, *British Immigrants in Industrial America, 1790-1950* (Cambridge, Mass., 1953); C. K. Yearley, *Britons in American Labor (1820-1914)* (Baltimore, 1957); Brinley Thomas, *Migration and Economic Growth* (Cambridge, Mass., 1954); Arnold Schrier, *Ireland and the American Emigration* (Minneapolis, 1958); Richard H. Heindel, *The American Impact on Great Britain, 1898-1914* (Philadelphia, 1940); Ingrid Semmingsen, *Veien mot Vest* [The Way West] (2 vols., Oslo, Norway, 1941, 1950).

[18] Edward N. Saveth, "The Immigrant in American History," in *Commentary*, II (August 1946), 180-85. See also Dr. Saveth's valuable *American Historians and European Immigrants, 1875-1925* (New York, 1948). Since this paper was written, a new one-volume work on *American Immigration* by Maldwyn Allen Jones has appeared (Chicago, 1960) in the *Chicago History of American Civilization*. This is a useful survey, notable less for new research or fresh interpretations than for its objective handling of the story and its selective bibliography of American immigration.

If the great work seems remote, many lesser contributions are attainable. We need more area and group studies both for this country and for Canada—searches for "the leaven in the lump," with the use of interdisciplinary techniques. There is room for extensive additions to the edited letters, diaries, reports, memoirs, across the land and for many elements. We have all too little on the organizational life of immigrants. Pochmann's recent book suggests the need for more studies in literature, thought, and art, both as to the impact of European cultural influence on America and as to immigrant creative work—and I recall that for the Norwegians alone I once made up a list of about a hundred immigrant novels that had never been turned into English, and perhaps do not deserve translation, but are of cultural historical interest. We need more studies of the immigrant in the urban community, and we need to reappraise the immigrant factor in the history of the American frontier. Immigrant social and intellectual life is rich in research possibilities. Inevitably, migration, settlement, and the saga of people and the land as mirrored in fiction by Rölvaag's *Giants in the Earth* have attracted much attention, but many of the more genial and urbane aspects of immigrant transition invite research. Here, for instance, Henriette Koren Naeseth has given an illustration of illuminating work worth doing for many nationalities in her monograph on the pioneer Swedish theater and drama in Chicago.[19] Emigration and immigration as described and interpreted in novels, plays, and short stories by authors both in the Old and New worlds invite the critical appraisal of historians who are not committed to mere quantitative techniques, but have an eye to those imaginative approaches that give new and readier understanding. We need to see Hans and Olaf, Pierre, Guiseppe, and Patrick as human beings, emigrants and immigrants, persons who are born, work, live, love, and die, moving with their material and cultural baggage from one world to another, changing in their ways and attitudes as their worlds change, and having impact

[19] *The Swedish Theatre of Chicago, 1868-1950* (Chicago, 1951).

on the societies they left and on those with which they merged their lives.

There are inviting opportunities in immigrant church history, education, the story of the press, folklore and folk arts, sports and amusements, labor and industry, the emigrant trade, the story of the immigrant second generation (to which the novelist Rölvaag gave attention after writing *Giants in the Earth*), the immigrant farm and farm community, politics, the migration of culture in its grass-roots sense, and the European backgrounds of ideas and institutions. We need more studies of the emigrants who, successful or unsuccessful in America, returned to their homeland, and here Theodore Saloutos, in his research on the Greeks who went back to Greece, has pioneered new paths.[20] We urgently need critical and thorough-going studies of many national elements that have not yet found historians of high scholarly quality, and this need is particularly compelling for the immigrants from the southern and southeastern parts of Europe, from Latin America, and from the vast world to the Far East. We need more emphasis than we have had on the recent periods of immigration. Interesting and illuminating for the full saga would be a pictorial history of American immigration. Rich illustrative materials are now available in such institutions as the Library of Congress, the Nebraska and Minnesota historical societies, the George Eastman House in Rochester, New York, and various college and special museums and libraries.

There is need, also, of viewing the migration both of people and of ideas in worldwide compass—migration from the Old World to the New not only, but back and forth in many parts of the world in this jostling, restless age. Nor is the migration merely that from country to country—my own studies have indicated a close relationship of emigration with extensive internal migration in the countries that poured emigrants into America in the nineteenth and twentieth centuries. The problems both of world migration and of internal shifts in the

---

[20] Theodore Saloutos, *They Remember America* (Berkeley, 1956).

countries of the Old World are too great and complex for treatment by our own historians alone. Scholars in many countries must cooperate if they are to deal adequately with the phenomenon of population movements in a vastly larger context than that simply of the immigrant influx into the United States.

The Hansen essay and the many books and innumerable articles that have appeared in the past two or three decades offer many other clues to research needed before we can fill out the general picture and pave the way to large surveys and interpretations. As in other areas of cultural history, guides to source materials can aid scholars in their own hunts for unused or little-used records and can mark out potential paths to new subjects of research. Scholars for the most part are their own pathfinders, but they do not spurn assistance. Now and then we fail to appreciate the richness of sources already collected and available. An illustration is afforded by Homer L. Calkin in an article that describes the research materials in the National Archives on Irish immigration and naturalization, the political significance of the Irish in America, their social and economic conditions, their relations with the homeland, and various other topics.[21] In the realm of printed materials, Dr. O. F. Ander has made available an impressive list of selected references on the cultural heritage of the Swedish immigrant which reveals how ample and varied the historical documentation can be for a single element in the population.[22]

The problem of publication confronts all scholars, in whatever field. Many major works on immigration have been brought out through university and other presses; and numerous articles have appeared in national and regional journals and in the organs of societies that focus their interest upon particular immigrant groups. How extended the opportunities are for essays and short documentary items even in the history of a single population element finds illustration in the work of

[21] "The United States Government and the Irish," *Irish Historical Studies,* IX (March, 1954), 28-52.
[22] *The Cultural Heritage of the Swedish Immigrant* (Rock Island, Ill., 1956).

the Norwegian-American Historical Association, which has published no fewer than twenty volumes of *Studies and Records* (and more than a score of other books) since it was founded in 1925.[23] Valuable as are such contributions for the national story, the importance of the total field and the mounting interest of American and European scholars suggest that the time may not be distant when a "Journal of Immigration" should be inaugurated. Such a journal could serve the useful purpose of bringing together general and special articles dealing with the immigrant in American life. Its special field could be that of American immigration from colonial times to the present, with due attention to Old World backgrounds and repercussions, but it could also grapple with emigration in its worldwide dimensions. Edited in accordance with rigorous critical standards, it could provide a forum for contributions that, by virtue of present circumstances, too often are restricted to narrow circles of readers. It could provide national and international encouragement to scholarship on the immigrant theme by bringing together studies of many areas, periods, elements, and problems. I do not doubt that, if a journal of such character came into being, scholars would provide it with rich content and competent editorial direction, with attention to good writing as well as to scholarly excellence.

[23] For an appraisal of the Association, see Franklin D. Scott, "Controlled Scholarship and Productive Nationalism," *Norwegian-American Studies and Records,* XVII (Northfield, Minn., 1952), 130-48.

THE SCIENTIST ON THE FRONTIER

JOSEPH EWAN

ROM THE parsonage of the Reverend Manassah Cutler in Ipswich and the plantation of Thomas Walter on the Santee River to the travels of Thomas Nuttall over the Oregon Trail in 1834 and of Charles Christopher Parry in Jefferson Territory at the Second Gold Rush, scientists have often been in the vanguard of the frontier movement. As the American historian Henry Nash Smith has expressed it, the scientists of the frontier "stand as symbols of that single dramatic gesture of expansion which has been the dominant rhythm of Western European civilization since the fifteenth century."[1] Smith recognizes four frontiers: the socio-political frontier, treated by Turner, often marked by colonization movements; the technical frontier, marked by the impact of technology on the less-advanced resident population; thirdly, the frontier, of special interest here, of objects "new-to-science," setting off the known forms of plants, animals, and minerals from the undescribed "new species"; and the frontier of scientific perception—Smith calls it 'scientific intention'—by which newly gained scientific knowledge will contribute to the development of new scientific concepts. In this last frontier area are such problems as the classification of organisms, the nature of cells, of processes, of life itself. This fourth frontier is one of depth, whereas the other three are geographic or spatial. It is noteworthy that, though these four frontiers do not always coincide in history, they often did fall together between 1820 and 1850, in the development of the American West and Southwest.

The scientists on the socio-political frontier were in closer touch with the intellectual centers of the Western World than most of their fellow frontiersmen. The concepts of nature were undergoing immense expansion and revision, and through the minds of the frontier scientists coursed the same ideas and questions that concerned their colleagues abroad or back on the Atlantic seaboard. These thoughts, unthinkable by their fellow frontiersmen, bound these men in a fraternity of spirit and supported them in extremity. In such men at their best we encounter a blend of the pathfinder's courage and the scientist's intellectual curiosity. We find men combining the qualities of a Vesalius and of a Coronado, of an Asa Gray and a Kit Carson.

The history of science, as Henry Sigerist once remarked, is the bridge between the humanities and science: "the time is past when historians could picture the history of mankind in the light of dynastic quarrels, of wars and peace treaties," yet "the history of science is a very young field of research that is cultivated by a handful of people only."[2] It is the purpose of this survey to glance at some already published biohistorical sketches which have contributed to American cultural history, and to take a longer look at the unpublished materials which await future historians in the deep deposits of our libraries and archives.

First, there is a group of Atlantic seaboard figures whose stories have been published or are presently in progress. Some

[1] "What Is the Frontier?" *Southwest Rev.* XXI (1935), 97-103.

[2] Henry E. Sigerist quoted by F. Verdoorn, *Chron. Bot.* VIII (1944), 433, "On the Aims and Methods of Biological History and Biography," a discussion of value to the student. George Sarton reiterated Sigerist's view in his *Guide to the History of Science* (Waltham, 1952), 65.

of these studies are oriented toward cultural history, but many of the investigators, as professional scientists, place their subjects under the microscope of narrow concern, with scarcely a hint of sociohistorical focus. In this review we shall begin with men who had a serious interest in what we may readily identify as scientific materials, passing over the earliest explorers who often made penetrating observations of natural history but whose approach was not orderly or calculated to systematize our knowledge. In this frame of reference perhaps the very first figure in America was the Reverend John Banister of Virginia, of the late seventeenth century, who will be the subject of attention somewhat later in this essay, falling as he does among those whose travels and writings are not yet in print.

The *Travels* of Peter Kalm, the "disciple" of Linnaeus, are source materials for Nova Caesaria, the New Jersey of the mid-eighteenth century. The Swedish government hoped through the introduction of the silkworm to found an industry in America, but Kalm's *Travels* proved to be a more enduring fabric than the silks of South Jersey. An annotated edition of his *Travels* was published by A. B. Benson in 1937, and Esther L. Larsen of Crown Point, Indiana, who has worked out several bypaths of Kalm's visit to this country, is engaged on a biography of the lynx-eyed visitor from Uppsala. Dr. Johann David Schoepf, age 25, came to America in 1777 as surgeon to the Ansbach troops, but stayed to travel and observe after the Revolution, returning to Europe in 1784; his *Reise* (1788) was edited by Alfred J. Morrison under the title *Travels in the Confederation* (1911).[3] Reverend Manassah Cutler, a colorful figure from several viewpoints, minister, naturalist, mountaineer, is now being studied by Lee N. Newcomer. Cadwallader Colden, who died in the year 1776 at the age of 88,

[3] Johann David Schoepf (1752-1800): see Max Meisel, *Bibliography of American Natural History* (New York, 1924-1929), 3:651; J. Ewan, "L'Activité des premiers explorateurs français dans le S. E. des Etats-Unis" in Centre National de la Recherche Scientifique, *Les Botanistes Français en Amérique du Nord avant 1850* (Paris, 1957), 39.

left a rich residue of scientific letters and papers, lectures, and scholarly treatises that are now under scrutiny by Harold S. Rand of Rochester and Siegfried B. Rolland of Wayne University.

Jacques Milbert[4] came from France to investigate natural history in 1815 and stayed seven years. He met men prominent in this country, collected materials for the Natural History Museum in Paris, sketched and described natural phenomena, geological, historical, and sociological. Yet very little is recorded of his visit; Max Meisel does not even mention him. Twelve letters written by him, 74 pages of letters addressed to him, and a 45-page catalogue of specimens await some investigator in Paris. Miss Constance D. Sherman, of the American Museum of Natural History, is translating his two-volume *Itineraire pittoresque*, 1827-1829, a sumptuous folio, to be seen in only a few libraries in this country. A contemporary with Milbert in New York was David Hosack, M.D., whom I often think of as the "Sir Joseph Banks of America." Dr. Hosack has been under study by Mrs. Christine Chapman Robbins of Bronxville.[5] Few studies of American naturalists compare with Francis Harper's on John and William Bartram for the minute analysis of surviving letters and records; his recently published 'Naturalists' Edition' of William Bartram's *Travels* (1958) documents not only a family, but an entire period. Harper's biography of William Bartram and his associates is nearing completion. Amos Eaton, the professor extraordinary of Albany, has been portrayed by Ethel M. McAllister (1941).

First professor of botany in the United States was Benjamin Smith Barton whose journal of his visit to Virginia in 1802 has been edited by W. L. McAtee. "The Natural Bridge is certainly a very great curiosity," wrote Professor Barton, "and will well reward the trouble of a visit to behold it." Barton continues:

[4] Jacques Gerard Milbert (1766-1840): W. J. Robbins, *Proc. Amer. Philos. Soc.* CI (1957), 365-66.
[5] David Hosack (1769-1835): C. C. Robbins, *Proc. Amer. Philos. Soc.* CIV (1960), 293-313.

"One of the most disagreeable circumstances respecting the different Springs is the great numbers of Flees about them. These vile insects are very common at most, if not all, the Virginia Watering Places. Mr. Jefferson informed me, that at the Springs, they are obliged to put walnut-leaves on the bedding to drive away the flees. Mr. Randolph says, it is a good practice to put sheep where flees are, to get rid of these insects; & that in the counties of Bath & Augusta the people even raise their houses in such a way, as to admit sheep under them. It is certain, he said, that the flees migrate into the wool of the sheep, and he suspects, that they are destroyed, owing to the grease of the wool. But flees (he said) abound in the fur of the "Hare" (our rabbit) and do not perish there, because the fur of this animal is very clear being without grease."[6]

Thomas Nuttall,[7] in several ways one of the most extraordinary men of nineteenth century science: botanist, ornithologist, conchologist, geographer, as well as artist, printer, professor, explorer, and author, is the subject of a full-length biography in preparation by Jeannette Graustein of New York City. Mark Catesby and John Abbot have both been followed in close detail by Elsa Gundrum Allen of Cornell University's Laboratory of Ornithology. Dr. Allen has published on Catesby,[8] and a full length biography of Abbot of Georgia is in press. Samuel Mitchill, contemporary of Hosack in New York, is the subject of a published thesis by Courtney Hall (1934). Henry Muhlenberg, the botanical star in the Pennsylvania

---

[6] Benjamin Smith Barton (1766-1815): W. L. McAtee, *Castanea: Jour. Southern Appalachian Bot. Club* III (1938), 85-117. Cf. also Whitfield J. Bell, Jr., *Early American Science: Needs and Opportunities for Study* (Williamsburg, Va., 1955), 45. Apparently overlooked by Bell and by F. W. Pennell, who made the most penetrating study of Barton, is his editing of J. H. Bernardin de Saint-Pierre's *Studies of Nature*, trans. Henry Hunter (Philadelphia, 1808), wherein Barton's initialed footnotes record a rich residue of philosophic observation of the period.

[7] Thomas Nuttall (1786-1859): Bell 68; R. G. Beidleman, *Proc. Amer. Philos. Soc.* CIV (1960), 86-100.

[8] Mark Catesby (1679-1749): Elsa G. Allen, *Trans. Amer. Philos. Soc.* n. s. XLI (1951), 463-78. For John Abbot (1751-1840?) see 543-49, and *Ga. Hist. Quar.* XLI (1957), 143-57.

firmament of Muhlenbergs, was a truly remarkable man in an era of notable men. When Alexander von Humboldt visited the United States he made a detour to Lancaster from Philadelphia to consult Henry Muhlenberg on botanical problems, especially on the taxonomy of grasses. His life has been briefly sketched by Paul Wallace (1950).

The role of François André Michaux in the development of forestry in this country has been traced by J. R. Schramm, the Canadian travels by Jacques Rousseau, and the cultural exchanges between America and France centering about the father, André, and son, by Gilbert Chinard. The journal of Charles Alexandre Lesueur has been painstakingly transcribed from the original at Le Havre by Madame Chinard and, when its editing has been completed, will be an important addition to our Mississippi Valley record from both the natural history and the social history viewpoints. Lesueur left a large portfolio of sketches, mostly made in the course of his travels; these have been enumerated by R. W. G. Vail (1938).

William Maclure, a friend of Francois Michaux and Lesueur, was a gentleman-scholar who invested a fortune in the works of several scientists and who participated actively in the New Harmony enterprise. His life is being chronicled by Miss Ludie Kinkead, curator of the Filson Club, Louisville, Kentucky. Charles Willson Peale, artist, naturalist, antiquarian, whose Philadelphia museum was a 'must' for every visitor to that city during the early decades of the last century, has been studied in detail by Charles C. Sellers (1947), and now Jessie Poesch has completed a full-length literary portrait of his talented son, Titian Ramsey Peale. The story of Thomas Say, an associate of Peale and Maclure in natural history and an Owenite of the New Harmony coterie when Lesueur was a resident there, has been told by Harry B. Weiss and Grace M. Ziegler (1931). More recently Margaret Cole has published in England *Robert Owen of New Lanark* (1953), providing more details regarding the social experiment on the Wabash.

Interest in Rafinesque has revived since T. J. Fitzpatrick published a working bibliography of the controversial genius in 1911. Charles Boewe of the University of Pennsylvania is pursuing the study of Rafinesque with the wide-angle lens of the social historian; he has reported on the voluminous manuscripts of Rafinesque (1958). Two dynamic figures of the nineteenth century were James Hall, geologist, and Asa Gray, botanist, of pivotal positions in their respective fields. Hall was state geologist of New York. His relations with the growth of American science have been told by his successor, John Mason Clarke of Albany (1923). The only botanist to win a pedestal in New York University's Hall of Fame is Asa Gray whose name will forever be associated with Harvard's role in botany. A. Hunter Dupree has traced Professor Gray's connections with a wide circle of contemporaries here and abroad in his recent full-length biography (1959).

Another group of studies has dealt with frontier scientists of the "plains and Rockies." We may mention very briefly: John Bradbury, investigated by Harold W. Rickett of the New York Botanical Garden; Edward Harris and Thaddeus Culbertson, Tixier, and Trudeau—all followed step by step by Professor McDermott. More recently he has edited, in collaboration with Kate L. Gregg, the story of the Wyoming hunting parties of Sir William Drummond Stewart, as chronicled by Matthew C. Field under the title *Prairie and Mountain Sketches* (1957).

The Italian Beltrami,[9] discoverer of the headwaters of the Mississippi in the early nineteenth century, has himself been rediscovered by his countrywoman, Dr. Wally B. Giacomini, in a memoir published in Bergamo in 1955. Dr. Jacob Schiel, who travelled with Capt. Gunnison in the Rockies, now speaks English in a translation recently prepared by T. N. Bonner (1959). The diaries of Charles Preuss, cartographer with Fremont, have been translated by the German scholars Erwin and Elizabeth Gudde (1958). Archaeologist Henry Rowe Schoolcraft is being scrutinized by Philip Mason. John Merle Coulter, botanist, who began a teaching career as an assistant

---

[9] Giacomo Costantino Beltrami (1779-1855): W. B. Giacomini, *Giacomo Costantino Beltrami* (Edizioni Orobiche, Bergamo, 1955); Meisel 3:536.

with the Hayden Survey, has been tracked by A. D. Rodgers III (1944), in one of a series of biographies of botanists. The photographer with the Hayden party, William Henry Jackson, has left us his autobiography, *Time Exposure* (1940), published in his 97th year! Hayden himself is now being surveyed with the completeness of a topographic map by two geologists working together, J. V. Howell and F. M. Fryxell. Hayden had been stimulated to take up geology by James Hall and thus the frontier of knowledge was carried west from New York state to the Rocky Mountains. Out of Hayden's work and that of his associates was established the United States Geological Survey.

Edward Palmer was addicted to an almost extinct vocation, the professional natural history collector. He was an ethnologist and poked into the byways of the Old Southwest. Useful far beyond the subject itself is Rogers McVaugh's life of Palmer (1956). Texas is fortunate for her biohistorian Samuel Wood Geiser, whose beautifully written human stories of her naturalists, Charles Wright, the Swiss Berlandier, and others, assembled in his *Naturalists of the Frontier* (ed. 2, 1948), delight the mind and warm the heart. Geiser's recent encyclopedic account of Texas scientists will be found an essential tool by the historian of the Southwest. Capt. R. B. Marcy, Josiah Gregg, John Wesley Powell, and A. W. Whipple have all been the subjects of biographies and a comprehensive survey of their role on the frontier has been provided by William H. Goetzmann in his *Army Exploration in the American West, 1803-1863* (1959).

On the Pacific Coast gathered a large group of argonaut scientists, beginning with the collector David Douglas, expertly reported by Athelstan Harvey (1947). Then came his hapless successor, John Jeffrey,[10] whose hazy life story has been recovered from Edinburgh archives by J. T. Johnstone. William Brackenridge, who travelled with Wilkes—"stormy petrel of

[10] John Jeffrey (1826-1854): J. Ewan, "San Francisco as a Mecca for Nineteenth Century Naturalists," in Calif. Acad. Sci., *A Century of Progress in the Natural Sciences, 1853-1953* (San Francisco, 1955), 1-63, Jeffrey on p. 52.

the Navy"—around the world, has been written about by several persons but not yet adequately placed in his kaleidoscopic setting. George Davidson of San Francisco has been portrayed by Oscar Lewis (1954); William Henry Brewer of the California State Geological Survey, whose keen observations of that state during its early decades is of greatest interest to the social historian, by F. P. Farquhar (1930, reissued, 1949); and John Xantus, Hungarian naturalist who pioneered in Baja California, by Henry Madden (1949). Three scientists whose histories are being written at the present time are Thomas Jefferson Howell of Oregon,[11] by Erwin Lange; Andrew Jackson Grayson,[12] the "Audubon of the Pacific," by Lois Chambers Taylor Stone of Berkeley; and the little-known Englishman Lorenzo Gordin Yates,[13] who came to California in 1851, by the paleontologist and biohistorian Charles L. Camp.

Now to turn to what we may call a "waiting list" of those frontier scientists who present ripe opportunities for the culture historian. We may flag them by nationalities; first the native Americans, then the British, the French, and, lastly, the German scientists on the frontier.

For Nova Scotia there is Titus Smith (1768-1850),[14] the "Dutch village philosopher," who portrays Nova Scotia at the turn of the nineteenth century. His biographical materials are preserved in the Provincial Archives at Halifax. Elisha Mitchell[15] was an omnivorous observer. His commentaries on the

---

[11] Thomas Jefferson Howell (1842-1912): E. F. Lange, *Sci. Mo.* LXXVII (1953), 198-204; see also A. L. Kibbe, *Afield with Plant Lovers and Collectors: Botanical correspondence of the late Harry N. Patterson with the great botanical collectors and distributors of America from 1870 to 1919* (Carthage, Ill., 1953), 468-73. Both of these have annoying typographical errors and a few factual lapses.

[12] Andrew Jackson Grayson (1819-1869): Ewan, "San Francisco," 50.

[13] Lorenzo Gordin Yates (1837-1909): James Britten, and George S. Boulger, *A Biographical Index of Deceased British and Irish Botanists,* ed. 2 (London, 1931), 337.

[14] Titus Smith (1768-1850): "Survey of the eastern and northern parts of the Province. In the Years 1801 & 1802 [etc.] by Titus Smith Jr., Halifax, 1857, ed. 3," 179 pp. Ms. no. 380 in Halifax archives.

[15] Elisha Mitchell (1783-1857): Journal, 1827-1828, ed. by Kemp P. Battle. James Sprunt, *Hist. Monog.* [Univ. North Carolina] no. 6: 1-73, 1905.

Carolina mountains of the last century and their piedmont villages may well prove the greatest legacy of a life marked by diffuse scientific and community interests.

Outstanding among American scientists for his sensitive observations, wide contacts, and travels here and abroad, was the Yale professor, founder and editor of the *American Journal of Science and Arts*, Benjamin Silliman.[16] With due acknowledgment of the late Dr. John Fulton's study of Silliman (1947) in collaboration with Elizabeth H. Thomson, abundant opportunities remain. The Yale archives house the Silliman papers, and his letters turn up literally all over the world, testifying to his immense energies. To sample Silliman let us select a few paragraphs from his *Tour between Hartford and Quebec in the Autumn of 1819* (New Haven, 1820):[17]

"First Impressions of Montreal. We mounted a steep slippery bank, from the river, and found ourselves in one of the principal streets of the city. It required no powerful effort of the imagination, to conceive that we were arrived in Europe. A town, compactly built of stone, without wood or brick, indicating permanency, and even a degree of antiquity, presenting some handsome public and private buildings, an active and numerous population, saluting the ear with two languages, but principally with the French—every thing seems foreign, and we easily feel that we are a great way from home." (195-96)

"We frequently observed, on the Sorel river, the French women, washing at the river's edge. The same employment is seen here before our windows. Sometimes the clothes are

[16] Benjamin Silliman (1779-1864): Meisel 1:230 and 3:655. In addition to "innumerable letters," Silliman left an unpublished, nine-volume autobiography entitled "Origin and Progress in Chemistry, mineralogy, and geology in Yale College and other places, with personal reminiscences (between 1857 and 1862)"; he also left the manuscript volumes of his travel diaries; his account books for his first trip abroad and the early years of his professorship, a volume on the foundation of the Trumbull Art Gallery, as well as a seventeen-volume daybook (1840-1864). John F. Fulton and Elizabeth H. Thomson, *Benjamin Silliman, 1779-1864, Pathfinder in American Science* (New York, 1947), viii.

[17] *Tour between Hartford and Quebec in the Autumn of 1819* (New Haven, 1820); 2d. edn. "with corrections and additions" (New Haven, 1824). Page references in text are to the first edition.

placed on boards, in the river, and pounded; and, at other times, the women dance on them, dashing the water about like ducks, and seemingly as much for frolic as the work. All these employments, are attended with much vociferation, and contribute to give life and interest to the quiet scenes of a great inland water." (201)

In remarking on the progress of the churches and the erection of "three pretty modern churches" Silliman has this to say:

"We are not, however, to infer that increased resources, nor additional zeal for religion has reared these edifices; it was the effect of local jealousies, as to the place, where a new house should be built, and how often, in our New England villages, do we see this circumstance produce the same result, adding to the beauty, but, perhaps, not always to the harmony and piety of the neighborhood." (31)

In the West there are three Americans whose commentaries will reward the historian of culture: Lester Frank Ward,[18] already noticed for his social philosophies—though scarcely an "American Aristotle," I would protest—traveled in Utah in the last half of the nineteenth century and kept lively notes on men and marriages, minerals and mirages. Ward was fond of names on the land, and I read his specimen labels with undisguised pleasure: Twelve Mile Creek, Rabbit Valley, Dirty Devil River, The Button, and Aquarius Plateau. Then there is the geologist Benjamin Franklin Shumard,[19] who stirred Texas to an awareness of her mineral wealth only to be victimized by political corruption. The ornithologist Henry W. Henshaw[20] has left an intimate autobiography that tells of his messmate years with the governmental Bureau of Biological Survey and fills a long chapter in the history of our emerging policies on

[18] Lester Frank Ward (1841-1913): J. Ewan, *Rocky Mountain Naturalists* (Denver, 1950), 331. See Bernhard J. Stern, ed., *Young Ward's Diary* (N. Y., 1935), covering years 1860-1870. Unfortunately Ward's second wife destroyed his diary, 1870-1913, which covered his western experiences, "lest lapses of loyalty to her be disclosed" *teste* Stern.

[19] Benjamin Franklin Shumard (1820-1869): Meisel 1:230 and 3:654; S. W. Geiser, *Southwest Rev.* XVI (1930), 134-35 and *Field and Lab.* XXVII (1959), 203.

[20] Henry Wetherbee Henshaw (1850-1930): Ewan, "San Francisco," 51.

wild life and forest conservation. In the West first with the Wheeler Survey, Henshaw in later years loved the unspoiled wilds of Arizona as he disliked the governmental halls of Washington.

Of the British scientists on the frontier, first in time came the Reverend John Banister[21] whose early death at 38 was a real loss, not only to biology and anthropology, but to cultural history. He botanized, collected, corresponded, sketched, wrote, and preached, and he left accounts—only partially put into print by others—of Virginia's plants, insects, shells, rocks, and Indians. Defying Rousseau's maxim that "the man who rings the bell cannot march in the procession," with Mrs. Ewan's assistance I have edited an overlooked Banister manuscript of 1679-1692. Here are some Banister bits:

"Virginia is a country naturally so fertile, that it does or might be made to yield anything that may conduce to ye pleasure or necessity of life: but ye great crops of Tobacco some strive to make, and ye number of Planters which daily increases, and more by reason of a silly, fond, and withall a proud humour that generally possesseth ye poorer sort of people (as it is reported of ye Muscovites) that they had rather see their children starve at home, than put them out to learn anything abroad: These things, I say, hinder its improvement, for all arts & trades, if not propagated by communicating them to others, die with, if not before their masters. . . . Their [Indians] food is fish & flesh of all sorts, and that which participates of both, ye Beaver & Turtle, they reckon a delicate meat, which ye Dutch in ye Island of St. Helens prefer before Eeles; & they highly esteem ye flesh of snakes, especially that of ye Rattlesnake, no part of which inwardly taken is dangerous . . . altho its poyson be so deadly, when by biting or otherwise it is injected into ye wound & mixed with ye blood. I have known English as well as Indians dress & eat them, & not a few that have taken out ye heart of this irritated & enraged creature,

[21] John Banister (1654-1692): *DAB;* Meisel 1:162 and 3:724; J. E. Dandy, *Sloane Herbarium* (London, 1958), 84-87.

& swallowed it still palpitating, which I suppose common practice of ye natives; not their own experience, has made them to think a great cordial. . . . The women plant and tend ye corn, dress skins, tote, that is carry burdens, and do all drudgery both at home and abroad: ye men do little or nothing but hunt. They say we English are fools for 3 things; viz. for not making our wives work, eating with little spoons, & not always going with a gun; for they think themselves undrest & not fit to walk abroad, unless they have their gun on their shoulder, & their shot bag by their side."

Contemporary with Joseph Priestley, who died in Northumberland, Pennsylvania, in 1804, was Dr. John Coakley Lettsom,[22] whose American contacts were both numerous and important. Lettsom's letters to and from his American scientific friends—Waterhouse, Nathan Smith, Benjamin Rush, Cullen, James Mease, Samuel Mitchill, William Thornton, and others —are replete with lively wit and pungent analysis. Better known is the geologist Charles Lyell,[23] who visited the United States on three different occasions, in 1842, 1846, and 1852, and reported on the first two visits. What ever became of the journal of his third visit? In Lyell's unpublished letters back to America, and those circulated among his British colleagues regarding America, I've found the same honest estimate that he left us in his *Travels*. Lyell's contacts with James Hall, published by Clarke, bear witness to the lively competition that flourished in American laboratories and lecture rooms, and the impact of a foreign mentor on our growing science and public affairs.

In this same period came the botanist William Henry Harvey,[24] who visited botanists and "attractions" all the way

[22] John Coakley Lettsom (1744-1815): Britten and Boulger 186; J. J. Abraham, *Lettsom: His life, times, friends, and descendents* (London, 1933).

[23] Charles Lyell (1797-1875): Britten and Boulger 795; though recent books devoted to Darwin, Huxley, and Gray introduce Lyell, there is no modern biography. See also E. G. Conklin, *Proc. Amer. Philos. Soc.* XCV (1951), 220-22.

[24] William Henry Harvey (1811-1866): Britten and Boulger 141; John Hutchinson, *A Botanist in Southern Africa* (London, 1946), 585-86; R. Lloyd Praeger, *Some Irish Naturalists* (Dundalk, 1949), 98.

from Quebec, Niagara Falls, and Cambridge to Charleston, and made a four-week trip to Key West for algae. His letters are jolly, frank, and full of the contemporary scene. He wrote to his British colleague William Jackson Hooker, that he "was not quite Yankeefied yet, though [he had] made many good friends at the other side." The Harvey-Hooker correspondence is recommended. Somewhat earlier, in 1837-38, the Oxford professor of botany, Charles Daubeny,[25] came to the United States and "printed for private circulation only" his *Journal* of his tour in an edition of 100 copies. When he visited Charleston in January, 1838, Professor Daubeny remarked that "Southern men are in general not much burdened with religion; they contribute indeed to churches, but do not attend them." Daubeny wrote to Hooker from Oxford, March 4, 1843, upon the posting of a copy of his *Journal* to Hooker, remarking at that time, "I fear you will find the botanical notices scant. The fact was I am distracted by too many objects." So, you see, Daubeny is short on botany, long on cultural history.

Better known to the world of English literature than to science and history is the name of Gosse. Philip Henry Gosse,[26] father of Edmund Gosse, came to America in 1839 and took a country schoolmaster's seat in Alabama. He stayed only one year, depressed by the socioeconomic climate. His account, published twenty years later, is one of the most interesting commentaries on the ante bellum South, delineating as it does a tapestry of rural life, with incidental notes on natural history. The book is scarce today and might well be reprinted, with annotations. Peter Brannon, for many years Alabama state archivist, has assembled a vast array of memorabilia bearing on Gosse's visit and they should be consulted in any attempt to do the story full justice.

[25] Charles Giles Bridle Daubeny (1795-1867): Britten and Boulger 85, where no mention is made of his *Journal of a Tour through the United States . . . 1837-8* (Oxford, 1843).

[26] Philip Henry Gosse (1810-1888): Britten and Boulger 126, where *Letters from Alabama (U.S.) chiefly relating to Natural History* (London, 1859) is not mentioned; bibliographical notes by D. W. Tucker, *Jour. Soc. Bibliog. Nat. Hist.* III (1957), 223-29.

Also in the nineteenth century came Alfred Newton, William A. Bell, C. C. Parry, Andrew Murray, George Bennett, and General Strachey. The Cambridge ornithologist Newton[27] arrived in New Orleans in 1857 and travelled as far as Harvard yard to meet Agassiz. Newton's letters and journal should be sought. William A. Bell,[28] associate of General William Palmer, founder of Colorado Springs, while hardly a scientist, worked closely with several scientists and made some collections himself. His multifarious activities in Colorado, chiefly in railroading, ranching, and commerce, took him up and down the Rockies. Bell's English friend in botany, C. C. Parry,[29] must have aided him from his first year's residence in Colorado. Bell's *New Tracks in North America* (1869) would naturally constitute the centerpiece of any portrait of the "English gentleman of wealth and enterprise." Parry's place in cultural history has not yet been marked. Like Brewer of California, Dr. Parry saw everything that flowered, hatched, prospected, fought, failed, triumphed, died, or rose again in Colorado's mining years. And, better, Parry dearly loved to write informal, sometimes elegant accounts of all this for his cronies, a few relatives, and scientific associates around the world. He also wrote for the press, and these newspaper accounts if collected would present a wonderful kaleidoscope of Colorado, Utah, and California from the Mexican Boundary Survey down to the 1890's. Listen to this as he describes his approach to the Rockies:

"Near the base of the mountains, smooth, grassy swells,

27 Alfred Newton (1829-1907): Meisel 3:630; J. A. Allen, *Auk* XXIV (1907), 365-66; W. H. Hudleston, *Ibis*, ser. 9, II (1908), suppl. 107-116, with portr.; W. H. Mullens and H. Kirke Swann, *Bibliography British Ornithology* (London, 1917), 442-48; A. F. R. Wollaston, *Life of Alfred Newton* (London, 1921).

28 William Abraham Bell (1841-1921): Ewan, *Rocky Mountain Naturalists*, 160.

29 Charles Christopher Parry (1823-1890): Ewan, *Rocky Mountain Naturalists*, 34-44; E. D. Ross, *Miss. Valley Hist. Rev.* XXVII (1940), 435-41; "The Far West, Its external features and natural resources. First impressions of Rocky Mountain scenery" *Chicago Evening Journal*, Dec. 30, 1863, "written for the Journal."

gigantic in comparison with the undulations met with on the great plains, give a foretaste of the ruder character of scenery soon to be experienced. Projecting masses of dark-colored rock frown upon the traveler as he enters the rude defiles by which the traveled roads penetrate the mountain range. The view is soon shut in by rocky walls on either hand, and irregular broken slopes, scatteringly timbered by pine and spruce, occupy the contracted horizon. . . .

"Far from civilized haunts, you feel like treading in a world only partly finished, and as ever and anon the rude miners shanty or the wayside tavern comes into view, you almost expect to hear some strange dialect and foreign accent issue from the uncouth lips that greet you. . . . With a gradually increasing elevation, the traveler soon begins to experience some of the effects of a rarified air. This is first noticed by an unwonted shortness of breath, and an involuntary tendency to prolonged inspiration and forcible expansion of the chest, thus by an increased bulk endeavoring to make up for the diminished density. In climbing up any steep ascent, a panting breath, swollen veins, and occasional bleeding at the nose, require frequent and prolonged pauses, such as are not laid down in the ordinary works on punctuation. To a person in health, nature soon adapts herself to this condition of a rarified atmosphere, the lungs expand to take in a larger bulk of air, the muscles acquire vigor by exercise, and thus give tone to the circulating vessels, while a steady coolness of the atmosphere, and that exhilaration of the animal spirits that generally attend outdoor life makes ample amends for other deficiencies. This fact, together with the absence of the more common enervating influences of civilized life, will account for the usual degree of health experienced by the mountain *voyageur*."

As for Andrew Murray,[30] who came in 1873, and George

[30] Andrew Murray (1812-1878): Britten and Boulger 225; letters, Brigham, Utah, May, 1873, and London, 23 Feb. 1874 (Brit. Mus. Nat. Hist., autograph coll., Bot. Dept.); M. M. Carpenter, *Amer. Midl. Nat.* XXXIII (1945), 73 and L (1953), 316.

Bennett,[31] in 1877, no search has been made for journals and letters bearing on their American sojourns. They give promise of materials, for Murray visited Utah, and Bennett, a physician who had visited Ceylon at fifteen and lived many years in Australia, crossed the United States en route to England. General Richard Strachey,[32] engineer, was in Tibet in 1848, and in 1877 accompanied Joseph Dalton Hooker to America, visiting Colorado, Utah, and the Pacific Coast. He was en route to India, and, like Dr. Bennett, saw the world with the objectivity of a scientist. He was a longtime friend of Hooker and his letters are at Kew.

Some of the French scientists, like their German colleagues, were Forty-Eighters, influenced by Louis Agassiz and his resounding success in America. Jules Marcou[33] arrived in 1848, accompanied Lieut. Whipple as geologist, did bedrock work on several problems in stratigraphy, but met suspicions, jealousy, and governmental dishonesty. Marcou's position is controversial, a tangled plot for the detective. Prof. Arnold Guyot[34] of Princeton also arrived in America in 1848. His geological forays in Colorado of the 1870's, often with students, read like good hunting parties. Unlike Marcou, Professor Guyot left a coterie of admiring friends, and whereas James Dwight Dana flayed Marcou in print, he wrote a warm obituary of Guyot. With Guyot came Leo Lesquereux,[35] geologist, paleontologist, moss specialist, later in the West with the Hayden Survey. He travelled in Alabama, Tennessee, and Georgia in 1850, and wrote an account for his native Swiss

[31] George Bennett (1804-1893): Britten and Boulger 29; H. M. Whittell, *Literature of Australian Birds: a History and Bibliography of Australian Ornithology* (Perth, 1954), 49-50.
[32] Richard Strachey (1817-1908): Ewan, *Rocky Mountain Naturalists*, 316.
[33] Jules Marcou (1824-1898): Ewan, *Rocky Mountain Naturalists*, 258; G. P. Merrill, *First Hundred Years of American Geology* (New Haven, 1924), 678-81 *et passim.*
[34] Arnold Henry Guyot (1807-1884): Meisel 1:190; Ewan, *Rocky Mountain Naturalists*, 220-21.
[35] Charles Leo Lesquereux (1806-1889): Ewan, "Explorateurs Francais," 36; Merrill, 383-84 *et passim;* W. C. Darrah, *Harvard Bot. Mus. Leaflet* II (1934), 113-19.

town's paper; this has never been translated. Lesquereux, deaf from early manhood, with a poor command of English, "lived," he said, "with nature, the rocks, the trees, the flowers. They know me. I know them. All outside are dead to me." Yet his observations, made with the eyes of a microscopist, are penetrating, if unsocial.

Jules Remy[36] presents one of the most interesting figures among the Frenchmen in America, yet little has been written in a connected way of Remy's travels and observations. His *Journey to Great-Salt-Lake-City* (London, 1861), translated from the original French narrative of the year before, is noticed by historians, but this is only an isolated chapter of a life spent in exploration, including expeditions to the Hawaiian Islands, West America, and the Andes, before and after 1855, the year he visited the Mormons. He was evidently a professional collector for the Natural History Museum of Paris, and there his letters and journals, almost wholly unworked, will have to be sought.

Of all French frontier scientists, Gerard Troost,[37] says Geiser, "deserves a place beside Rafinesque. . . . He lacked the coruscating genius and the multifaceted type of mind of Rafinesque; but he had staying power and enduring patience." A naturalist interested in geology, conchology, paleontology, Troost was a linguist, book collector, member of many foreign academies, influential teacher at the University of Nashville, and the author of forty-five published papers. He seems to have left little in the line of narrative, but his letters should be gathered and would reach back to his years with William Maclure at Philadelphia, with Robert Owen at New Harmony, and to his death in 1850, the year of the closing of the University of Nashville.

The Germans congregated at a few frontier outposts. Out-

---

[36] Ezechiel Jules Remy (1826-1893): Ewan, *Rocky Mountain Naturalists*, 288; Ewan, "San Francisco," 58.

[37] Gerard Troost (1776-1850): Ewan, "Explorateurs Français," 39; Merrill 111 *et passim;* S. W. Geiser, *Naturalists of the Frontier*, ed. 2 (Dallas, 1948), 261-263 *et passim.*

standing was Dr. George Engelmann[38] whose long residence in St. Louis gave scientific recognition to the city on two continents. Humanitarian that he was, scientifically trained, patient and scholarly, his papers and letters will surely yield much of value to the social historian. Perhaps the very embarrassment of riches has stayed the hand of Engelmann's Boswell? Less known, but hardly less exciting, was August Fendler,[39] for whom we have enough of a record, salvaged by William M. Canby, to whet our appetite. The manuscript of Fendler's *Mechanics of the Universe* (1876) is preserved in the archives of the Smithsonian Institution Library.

Three other Germans with scientific tastes were associated with St. Louis: Wislizenus, Bischoff, and Geyer.[40] Wislizenus is fairly well known, but I have always wondered about the diary or letters bearing on his early trip into the Jackson Hole. Judging from his published accounts, this voyageur piece might prove extremely interesting, though the record may have been abbreviated under the difficult conditions of travel. Bischoff is little explored. He was evidently something of a professional collector, but less methodical than most. That Bischoff travelled in Indian Territory in its frontier years makes the search alluring. Charles Geyer's account of the Pacific Northwest, locked in difficult German script, should prove a notable complement to the Matthew Field and Sir William Drummond Stewart materials.

Biographically speaking, Ferdinand Rugel[41] is himself a frontier today; we have some personal record of his travels in

[38] George Engelmann (1809-1884): Ewan, *Rocky Mountain Naturalists*, 204; anon. in St. Louis *Daily Globe-Democrat* for Dec. 30, 1900, with unusual, though poor, portrait; Mary J. Klem in *Trans. Acad. Sci., St. Louis* XXIII (1914), 116-19.

[39] Augustus Fendler (1813-1883): Ewan, *Rocky Mountain Naturalists*, 207; see Susan Delano McKelvey, *Botanical Exploration of the Trans-Mississippi West, 1790-1850* (Jamaica Plain, 1955), 1022, for correction and additions.

[40] Frederick Adolphus Wislizenus (1810-1889): Ewan, *Rocky Mountain Naturalists*, 207; Ferdinand Bischoff (d. *post* 1871): *ibid.*, 165; Karl Anton Geyer (or Charles Andreas Geyer) (1809-1853): *ibid.*, 214; McKelvey, 770-91 *et passim*.

[41] Ferdinand Rugel (1806-1879): S. W. Geiser, *Field and Lab.* XVI (1948), 113-19 and XXVII (1959), 190.

Tennessee, Alabama, Georgia, and Florida, where he collected natural history specimens. For each of these specimens he prepared voluminous notes; I have puzzled over many of these in the British Museum (Natural History) and feel sure that were we successful in locating an intact fieldbook or letters written in the field the record would be both novel and notable. Rugel wandered fearlessly in the Florida hinterland and I marvel that he missed the Seminole arrows that felled his countryman, Leitner, before him. For Rugel materials, search may well be made among German records in St. Louis, in Geneva where his patron lived, and perhaps in Texas where his children settled.

Three Pacific Coast figures, frontiersmen all, await the historian's attention. They are Deppe, Purpus and Richthofen. Ferdinand Deppe[42] hides behind herbarium labels in European museums. One label, that of *Selaginella californica,* reads simply "California." It is a diminutive moss-like plant that almost surely came from Hawaii (or Vera Cruz?) and has never been recollected! The German professional collector went to Mexico with the physician Christian Schiede very soon after the English had penetrated a country previously inhospitable to foreigners. Together they ascended the volcano of Orizaba. Later we find Deppe, like his fellow countryman Eduard Vischer, an agent for a trading house in Mexico, plying his wares in California. But the fragments are only tempting and we should like to find the journals, letters, or manuscripts that might present, in the words of Henry Madden, "a careful and perceptive recording of things seen, a reasonably imaginative treatment of things felt but not seen."

Carl Albert Purpus[43] was an educated German who ventured

---

[42] Ferdinand Deppe (1794-1867): Ewan, "San Francisco," 47; McKelvey 426, 649, and 738; A. H. G. Alston, *Bull. British Mus.* (Nat. Hist.), *Botany I* (1955), 239-40; H. M. Madden in *German Travellers in California* (San Francisco, 1958) does not mention Deppe; Gustave O. Arlt, *Ferdinand Deppe's Travels in California in 1837* (Los Angeles, 1953), has introductory notes by Glen Dawson.

[43] Carl Albert Purpus (1851-1941): Ida Langman, *Revista Soc. Mex. de Hist. Nat.* X (1949), 334-336; Ewan, *Rocky Mountain Naturalists*, 285.

into the wastes of southern Nevada when the desert ranges were unmapped. Later he explored in out-of-the-way spots in Mexico and kept in touch with T. S. Brandegee, the San Diego botanist, who described his novelties. Baron Ferdinand Richthofen,[44] geologist, came to California in 1862 from China. He was bent on studying volcanic phenomena, met Whitney of the California State Survey, for whom he had warm admiration, and together they planned a geological survey of China, a land the Baron had previously come to know well. Richthofen wrote long letters to Whitney from China in later years and these were edited and published by Whitney, but I believe this is merely a beginning.

Again and again my remarks upon a frontier scientist have concluded with the note that we have found, to borrow a geologist's word, an outcrop, less often a truly rich vein, a lode. Now we go afield with the hammer of persistence (and, perhaps, something of a map?).

[44] Ferdinand Paul Wilhelm von Richthofen (1833-1905): Ewan, "San Francisco," 58.

Postscriptum:

Fresh basemarks include:

(p. 85) G. F. Frick and R. P. Stearns, *Mark Catesby: The Colonial Audubon* (Urbana, 1961).

(p. 86) Jessie Poesch, *Titian Ramsey Peale, 1799-1885, and His Journals of the Wilkes Expedition* (Amer. Philos. Soc. Memoirs LII, 1961, 214 pp.).

(p. 86) John Bachman (1790-1874) of Charleston, friend of Audubon: C. H. Neuffer, *Christopher Happoldt Journal. His European Tour with the Rev. John Bachman (June-December, 1838)* (Charleston, 1960).

(p. 88) John Wesley Powell: Elmo Scott Watson, *The Professor Goes West* (Bloomington, Ill., 1954).

(p. 88) Clarence King (1842-1901): Thurman Wilkins, *Clarence King* (New York, 1958).

FOLKLORE AND CULTURAL HISTORY

RICHARD M. DORSON

T HE DRAMATIC possibilities for folklore research within
the frame of American cultural history are best visual-
ized in the light of European achievements in folklore
study. In Europe "folklore" got its name in 1846 and
gained its status in the second half of the nineteenth century. Italy, France, and England had their day, when their
private scholars attained international distinction, and now
Finland, Sweden, Ireland, Germany, and Russia take the lead
in folklore activities, their governments all actively supporting
the cause of folklore.

Finnish nationalism runs parallel to the evolving science of
folklore, which developed from the collecting of Kalevala runes
and charms by Elias Lönnrot into a nationally sponsored
Finnish Literature Society in 1831. In collecting folklore the
Society also sought to preserve the ancient language and
poetry. In 1935, after a century of collecting, a new competition netted 133,000 items. The folklore archives of the Society
contain a million and a quarter items, contributed by thousands
of citizens from all social classes, and indexed on 275,000
cards.[1] From the Finnish scholars has come the so-called

historical-geographical method, practiced by most leading folklorists today, who compare hundreds of texts of a single tale or ballad to trace its original starting point and subsequent wanderings. This method is demonstrated in an international series of renown, the Finnish Folklore Fellows Communications.

The Irish Folklore Commission, organized in 1935, has similarly served the movement of Irish nationalism and the revival of Gaelic speech. Its intensive collecting program and corps of full-time and part-time field workers have accumulated in the Irish archives over a million pages of manuscript, largely in Gaelic. To assist the collectors, an exhaustive *Handbook of Irish Folklore* provides a questionnaire into every conceivable aspect of traditional life in Ireland. Sean O'Sullivan adapted this handbook from the classification system developed by the Swedes from their documents in four vast folklore archives at Stockholm, Uppsala, Lund, and Gothenburg, and the artifacts in their eight hundred provincial and urban folk museums.[2]

In Russia, where the scientific collection of *byliny* from individual narrators began in 1831 with P. V. Kireyevsky, the Soviet Union has fully exploited propaganda potentialities in folklore materials. By party decree in 1936 the academic folklorists openly recanted the bourgeois theory that folklore filtered down to the working people from the upper class, and professed the new gospel, that the farm and factory workers have created the songs of protest and the legends of anti-Tsarist and revolutionary heroes which are the genuine Soviet folklore. The Party recognizes folklore both as a weapon in the class conflict and as a force for national unity among the diverse peoples of the Soviet Union. Collective farm workers

[1] Jouko Hautala, "The Folklore Collections of the Finnish Literature Society," *Studia Fennica*, V, no. 6 (1947), 197-202. See also, by the same author, "The Folklore Archives of the Finnish Literature Society," *Studia Fennica*, VII, no. 2 (1957), 3-36.

[2] A good discussion of the work of the Irish Folklore Commission by Sean O'Sullivan is in *Four Symposia on Folklore*, ed. Stith Thompson (Bloomington, Ind., 1953), pp. 2-16; Sigurd Erixon talks about the Swedish folk-life museums, *ibid.*, pp. 175-81.

are encouraged to compose songs. For example, a brochure published by the Political Division of the Starozhilov machine-tractor station in 1934 and presented to the Writers' Congress proudly announced that thirty-six of the thirty-eight collective farms served by their station had produced authors or collectors of their folk-poetry.[3] Quite apart from their propaganda use of folklore, the Russian-Soviet concern with the artistry and biography of the individual narrator and folk poet far eclipses comparable studies in other countries.

In most European states one or more professorships of folklore or institutes of folklore and folk music exist. Cooperative scholarship has produced such monuments as the *Handwörterbuch des deutschen Aberglaubens*, the ultimate reference on folk beliefs.[4] In August, 1959, the vitality of European interest in folklore received a new proof in the successful first International Folktale Congress held at Kiel and Copenhagen. Some three hundred folktale scholars attended, including the largest delegation from the United States yet to attend a European folklore meeting.

The folklore situation in the United States presents a striking contrast to the picture in Europe. Instead of a constant growth of folklore organization, interest has surged and ebbed. A wave of enthusiasm followed the founding of the American Folklore Society in 1888, ten years after the birth of the English society. A dozen branch societies held meetings in various cities. An especially active group met in Boston and Cambridge, where Francis James Child issued his famous edition of the English and Scottish ballads, and even a Harvard Folklore Club thrived from 1894 to 1900. During the 1880's and 1890's a Negro folklore branch met regularly at Hampton Institute, Virginia, and published summaries of papers and the texts of Negro folklore in the *Southern Workman*. A rival organization, the Chicago Folk-Lore Society, came into ex-

[3] Y. M. Sokolov, *Russian Folklore*, tr. Catherine R. Smith (New York, 1950), p. 26.
[4] In ten volumes, edited by E. Hoffman-Krayer and Hans Bachtold-Staubli (Berlin and Leipzig, 1927-42).

istence in 1891 under the leadership of Lieutenant Fletcher S. Bassett, U. S. N., and established its own branches in various states. George Washington Cable, for instance, was appointed head of the Louisiana branch of the Chicago Folk-Lore Society! Bassett edited one issue of a journal, *The Folk-Lorist*, and arranged an impressive international folklore congress in 1893 in conjunction with the Chicago World's Fair.[5]

Yet these promising beginnings all faded out. By the turn of the century the local branches of the American Folklore Society, and the Chicago Folk-Lore Society had dissolved. After the death of its first editor, William Wells Newell, in 1900, the *Journal of American Folklore* fell for the next forty years into the hands of professional anthropologists, to whom folklore was necessarily a secondary interest.

During the 1920's and 1930's a new trend developed, as folksong collectors followed the exciting vistas opened up by John Lomax and Cecil Sharp. Volumes of Child ballads and cowboy, lumberjack, and Negro folksongs rolled from the press. Reed Smith in South Carolina, H. M. Belden in Missouri, Arthur Kyle Davis in Virginia, and Phillips Barry in New England made solid contributions to the young literature of folksong in America.[6]

The 1940's and 1950's witnessed a spurt of interest in the folktale, and from the southern Appalachians and the Ozarks the collections of Richard Chase, Vance Randolph, Leonard Roberts, and Marie Campbell have demonstrated that the elusive Märchen still abounded in parts of Anglo-Saxon United States.[7] With the vigorous pursuit of the two main forms of

[5] See "North American Folklore Societies" and "North American Folklore Societies: A Supplement," compiled by Wayland D. Hand, *Journal of American Folklore*, LVI (1943), 161-91, and LIX (1946), 477-94.

[6] Reed Smith, *South Carolina Ballads* (Cambridge, Mass., 1928); Henry M. Belden, *Ballads and Songs Collected by the Missouri Folk-Lore Society* (Columbia, Mo., 1940); Arthur K. Davis, *Traditional Ballads of Virginia* (Cambridge, Mass., 1929); Phillips Barry, ed., *Bulletin of the Folk-Song Society of the Northeast*, 1930-37.

[7] Richard Chase, *The Jack Tales* (Boston, 1943); Vance Randolph, *Who Blowed Up the Church House? and Other Ozark Folktales* (New York, 1952); Leonard W. Roberts, *South from Hell-fer-Sartin* (Lexington, Ky., 1955); Marie Campbell, *Tales from the Cloud-Walking Country* (Bloomington, Ind., 1958).

oral folklore, the ballad and the tale, a renewed enthusiasm for the whole field of folklore became apparent. Upon the initiation of the Southeastern Folklore Society in 1934 and its offspring, the *Southern Folklore Quarterly* in 1937, a host of state and regional folklore societies and publications came into being or revived, until at this writing about thirty such societies exist. The printed quarterlies, *Western Folklore, Midwest Folklore,* and *New York Folklore Quarterly,* are followed by various bulletins, newsletters, and leaflets, issued through photo-offset, mimeographing or similar process. The membership in these societies customarily consists of a few academic folklorists surrounded by amateur genealogists, folksingers, and hobbyists of various kinds. Meanwhile a generation of professional folklorists has emerged to take over the reins of the American Folklore Society. Since they have entered folklore from a variety of disciplines, chiefly English literature, modern languages, and musicology, their primary allegiance of course goes to their own professional organizations, and so the American Folklore Society is plagued by inconsistent attendance and lukewarm support. The Society now meets in alternate years with the Modern Language Association and the American Anthropological Association.

This rapid survey indicates the haphazard and rather unprofessional character of American folklore studies as compared with the European. The vast institutional archives in Europe, the team field trips, the salaried collectors, the cooperative encyclopedias, and the rival schools of interpretation so common abroad are yet to appear in the United States. An Archive of American Folksong does exist in the Library of Congress, but its recorded treasures are due chiefly to the collecting efforts of its first curators, Robert Gordon and the Lomaxes, and with its diminished budget and the loss of its director, the Archive is severely crippled. During the WPA days a folklore collecting program of a sort did develop under the Federal Writers Project, and its amateurish results at least suggested the accomplishments that might be attained with trained collectors. Actually the universities of Indiana and Pennsylvania and

U. C. L. A. have provided the chief institutional support for folklore curriculums, library collections, archives, and publications. The foundations are noticeably cool to folklore. "What is the real purpose in collecting all this folklore?" an official of one of the major foundations has asked.

For better or worse, the genius of American folklore study has so far expressed itself in the wayward, individual collector. The illustrious names are those of solitary figures, unacademic and nonprofessional, who drift into some special groove of interest and collect assiduously along that line, with little heed to other traditions, other collectors, or considerations of bibliography, scholarship, and theory. We think of John Lomax recording from cowboys and penitentiary Negroes; Vance Randolph scouring the Ozarks, and only the Ozarks, for all kinds of lore; Phillips Barry combing New England for folksong, and only for folksongs; George Korson, a Pennsylvania newspaperman, wondering if coal miners sang ballads; J. Frank Dobie, glamorizing the lore of the Southwest in volume after volume while scoffing at the "science of folklore." The most intensive single collection of American superstitions, *Folk-Lore from Adams County, Illinois*, was privately published in 1935 by an individual completely unknown to the folklore fraternity, Harry M. Hyatt. The most extensive collection of all kinds of folklore from a single state was gathered in North Carolina by a professor at Duke University, Frank C. Brown, who was so much the hobbyist that he could never classify, annotate, and steer his finds into print, and a group of specialists had to perform these tasks after his death.

In library studies as well as in field collections, the same individualistic tendency appears, even in works of an essentially cooperative nature. The one attempt at a comprehensive *Bibliography of American Folklore and Folk Song* (1951) was undertaken by a concert singer and music historian, Charles Haywood, who describes ruefully his painful attempts to transfer the contents of shoebox files directly into cold type; one box in fact was lost in a closet and never did turn up until after the book was published. As it stands, this gigantic work is indispensable, but it must also be used with extreme caution because of the numerous errors in citation and the loose definition of "folklore." This kind of task required a division of labor among specialists, or at least an advisory board. Yet when a group of experts was assembled for the *Standard Dictionary of Folklore, Mythology and Legend* (2 vols., 1949-50), the work proved to be uneven in coverage and content, and fell far short of expectations. The editor, Maria Leach, is a writer of children's folklore books.

Not only does folklore in America lack the hard core of professional scholars taken for granted in other disciplines, but the firmness of its data is softened by the widespread popular interest in folklore. Broad avenues of publication are wide open for so-called folklore materials. Compilers of treasuries, writers of juveniles, vendors of magazine and newspaper articles, cabaret folksingers, recreational camp directors, organizers of folk festivals, all these extend a warm welcome to whatever savors of folklore. The confusion between reworked and genuine folk materials is found even among scholars as well as in the general public, who are not particularly exercised about such matters.

By contrast with the lavish attention given half-baked folklore books aimed at the mass public, sometimes painstaking works of considerable merit are ignored. Two of the outstanding field collections done in the United States, both by highly competent folklore scholars, have remained unpublished dissertations for over a decade. The collection of tales and legends from the New Jersey piney country made by Herbert Halpert is a superb example both of fieldwork and annotation.[8] Also the collection of the tales told by and about Oregon Smith, and the analysis of his reputation and narrative techniques, undertaken by William H. Jansen, is a unique and valuable study.[9] But publishers, the university presses as well

[8] "Folktales and Legends from the New Jersey Pines; a Collection and a Study" (Indiana University dissertation, 1947).

[9] "Abraham 'Oregon' Smith: Pioneer, Folk Hero, and Tale-Teller" (Indiana University dissertation, 1949).

as the commercial firms, dislike variant texts, and, in fact, tend to disapprove of exact texts which reproduce the words of the narrator with all their repetitiveness and meanderings. (Stith Thompson tells how one well-known university press to whom he submitted his manuscript of *Tales of the North American Indians* asked him to rewrite the tales. Eventually Harvard University Press published the book in its original form.) Hence scholarly folklore studies cannot easily find their way into print, and when they do, too often attract relatively few readers. The most skillful American collection of the full range of a folklore within a limited area—and proper fieldwork can only cover a limited area—is *Folklore from the Schoharie Hills, New York* by Emelyn E. Gardner, a book that has received little acclaim.

A long step forward in American folklore studies can be made if folklore in the United States is seen in its proper relation to major periods and themes in American history which gave a special character to folklore in the United States, themes such as colonization, the westward movement, immigration, the Indian and the Negro, and even modern mass culture. A would-be American folklorist should divide his training equally between comparative folklore and the history of American civilization, as a preparation for his researches.[10]

The American folklorist who is exploring research opportunities must seek for raw materials in two directions, viz., printed (or manuscript) sources, and field collections. Both avenues offer many inviting leads.

Because printed sources can provide him with texts for the seventeenth, eighteenth, and nineteenth centuries, before field collecting was consciously undertaken, certain printed media are valuable and necessary to the worker in American folklore. Yet the folklorist usually feels ill at ease among newspaper files, while the literary historians who have stumbled on buried folk matter are frequently at a loss to recognize and identify their finds. The files of American newspapers from the mid-

[10] Richard M. Dorson, "A Theory for American Folklore," in *Journal of American Folklore*, LXXII (1959), 197-215.

1820's up to the mid-1850's are extremely rich in humorous and legendary tradition. Both ordinary newspapers, and the popular literary-sporting-family weeklies using a newspaper format, tapped oral tradition. The New York *Spirit of the Times* has been repeatedly mined and continues to yield new humorous tales and sketches of merit. At the American Antiquarian Society the author stumbled onto a good run of the *Spirit's* closest rival, the *Yankee Blade*—no complete file surviving—and excavated over a hundred Yankee yarns. The same library also possessed issues of similar still-rarer, short-lived comic weeklies, such as *Union Jack, Saturday Rambler,* and *Yankee Privateer.*[11] Ante-bellum papers filled with humorous lore are reported by Philip Jordan and George Kummer for Ohio, by Eugene Current-Garcia for Georgia, by Eston E. Ericson for North Carolina, and by Thomas D. Clark for Kentucky.[12] For the Far Western papers, the spadework of Duncan Emrich in Nevada, Randall V. Mills in Oregon, and Levette J. Davidson in Colorado has dug into profitable veins.[13]

The *Index to the Burlington Free Press in the Billings Library of the University of Vermont* (Montpelier, Vermont, 1940), compiled under the Federal Writers Project, lists well over a thousand entries under the headings "Stories," "Humor," and "Sketches." These stories traveled the rounds of the press, via the exchange, and for the decade 1848 to 1858 alone the *Free Press* listed more than three hundred exchange credits. Working from such a list, a roster of papers juicy in humor

[11] Comic tales from these four papers are reprinted in the author's *Jonathan Draws the Long Bow* (Cambridge, 1946).

[12] Philip D. Jordan, "Humor of the Backwoods, 1820-1840," *Mississippi Valley Historical Review,* XXV (1938), 25-38; George Kummer, "Specimens of Ante-Bellum Buckeye Humor," *Ohio Historical Quarterly,* LXIV (1955), 424-37; Eugene Current-Garcia, "Newspaper Humor in the Old South, 1835-1855," *Alabama Review,* II (1949), 102-21; Eston E. Ericson, "Folklore and Folkway in the Tarboro (N. C.) *Free Press* (1824-1850)," *Southern Folklore Quarterly,* V (1941), 104-25; Thomas D. Clark, *The Rampaging Frontier* (Indianapolis and New York, 1939).

[13] Duncan Emrich, ed., *Comstock Bonanza* (New York, 1950); Randall V. Mills, "Frontier Humor in Oregon and Its Characteristics," *Oregon Historical Quarterly,* XLIII (1942), 229-56; Levette J. Davidson, "Colorado Folklore," *Colorado Magazine,* XVIII (1941), 7-8, and with Forrester Blake, eds., *Rocky Mountain Tales* (Norman, Okla., 1947).

could be compiled, and those papers examined for folktales. Eventually, by analyzing the contents of key papers in each state and territory, the folktales current in the heyday of frontier humor would be very fully uncovered, for in those humor-hungry times it is safe to assume that a folk anecdote of any currency found its way into newsprint.

The technique for this research depends on familiarity with the type and motif indexes of folk literature. Those reports we now have on the ante-bellum newspapers and family weeklies usually fall short of the folklorist's demands in two main respects: they fail to reprint complete texts, and they fail to identify tales by type and motif numbers and known variants, and so to separate traditional from literary or factual narratives. One shining exception testifies to the rewards obtainable from the proper application of professional folklore methods. Arthur K. Moore, with the assistance of the folklorist William Hugh Jansen, published an article excerpting folktale texts from ante-bellum Louisiana newspapers.[14] In this batch of thirty-one reprinted texts, we find not only early nineteenth century recordings of well-known and still popular tall tales and sells, but also specimens of once familiar lying tales now vanished along with the circumstances that gave them point, such as the stories about violent "shakes" from fever and ague.

In combing these files, the folklorist can catch besides tall tales many other types of folk tradition: legends, beliefs, hoaxes, proverbs, conundrums, riddles, folk speech, rhymes, anecdotes, jokes. C. Grant Loomis has unearthed numerous items of humorous wordplay from these papers.[15] Other kinds of printed sources can also be searched for such traditions. Novels and short stories constitute a source for proverbial sayings of a bygone day, as Archer Taylor and B. J. Whiting have recently demonstrated in *A Dictionary of American Proverbs and Proverbial Phrases, 1820-1880.* Their sources included the humorists

[14] "Specimens of the Folktales from Some Antebellum Newspapers of Louisiana," *Louisiana Historical Quarterly,* XXXII (1949), 723-58.

[15] E.g., "Jonathanisms: American Epigrammatic Hyperbole," *Western Folklore,* VI (1947), 211-27.

of the Old Southwest, and Mark Twain, Cooper, Emerson, Irving, Lincoln, Lowell, Melville, and other, lesser authors. Under Archer Taylor's stimulus, a graduate student at Indiana University, Jan Brunvand, has just published *A Dictionary of Proverbs and Proverbial Phrases from Indiana Books Published before 1880*, based on the check list of Indiana novels by R. E. Banta. Reading through nearly one hundred of these often unreadable romances, Brunvand located some 1500 traditional sayings, comparisons, and miscellaneous phrases in a model study that can be emulated for other states. Wayland D. Hand, the compiler of the forthcoming dictionary of American popular beliefs and superstitions, has pleaded for listings of folk beliefs from early printed sources, in order to provide historical dates for the tens of thousands of superstitions which he is cataloguing and annotating from contemporary oral tradition. The long files of *The Old Farmer's Almanac* and *Nathan Daboll's Almanac*, to name two of the various almanac series available, would yield many examples of weather lore, folk medicine, signs, omens, taboos. Kittredge opened the door to this wealth of late colonial folk beliefs in *The Old Farmer and His Almanac;* now the folklorist seeks an orderly listing of all texts in chronological sequence. Texts of ballads, folk lyrics and folk hymns too can be recovered from periodicals, travel writings, and songsters, as Ralph Leslie Rusk and Harry Stevens have indicated.[16]

The copious bibliography of nineteenth-century songsters offers for the ballad specialist a hunting ground similar to that provided for the folktale specialist in the *Spirit of the Times* and other periodicals. Traditional and composed songs are printed promiscuously in these songbooks which, like folksingers, make no distinction between individual and folk pieces. Some traditional ballads originated with printed broadsides, and the several thousand entries given by Worthington Ford

[16] Ralph L. Rusk, *The Literature of the Middle Western Frontier*, 2 vols. (New York, 1926), I, 303-19; Harry R. Stevens, "Folk Music on the Midwestern Frontier 1788-1825," *Ohio Archaeological and Historical Society Publications*, LVII (1948), 126-46.

in his *Broadsides, Ballads, etc. Printed in Massachusetts, 1639-1800,* documents the abundance of printed ballad texts in colonial days.[17] The American jestbooks described by Harry B. Weiss will also furnish valuable texts for the research folklorist when he begins, as inevitably he must, to trace the antecedents of American jocular tales.[18] Vance Randolph has now under way an annotated collection of Ozark jokes.

One type of printed source which should prove highly rewarding in folklore materials is travel literature. A systematic examination of the titles listed in Wagner and Camp's bibliography of travel books for the Far West, or Thomas D. Clark's for the South, or Vail's for the old frontier, should yield volumes of social folklore—not merely texts, although they will appear, but also the settings in which folk custom and belief flourished.[19] Travelers are especially concerned with manners and customs, they listen to reports and stories of all kinds, and they devote full time to observation of local and regional culture. The traveler is a kind of amateur ethnographer. John Josselyn, the Englishman who reported on two seventeenth-century voyages to New England, may well deserve the title of America's first folklorist, so extensively did he note the legends of enchanted islands, mermen, sea-serpents, quill-throwing porcupines, and the marvelous properties of tobacco. In documenting the spread of Yankee humor through the West, Walter Blair relied principally on the accounts set down by travelers who kept hearing tales about the cunning of Yankee peddlers.[20]

[17] See the discussion of broadside printing in America in Malcolm G. Laws, *American Balladry from British Broadsides* (Philadelphia, 1957), pp. 44-49. The need for a classified index to traditional pieces in broadsides and songsters is expressed by D. K. Wilgus, *Anglo-American Folksong Scholarship Since 1898* (New Brunswick, N. J., 1959), p. 258.

[18] *A Brief History of American Jest Books* (New York: The New York Public Library, 1943), pp. 3-19.

[19] See R. W. G. Vail, *The Voice of the Old Frontier* (Philadelphia, 1949); Henry R. Wagner and Charles L. Camp, *The Plains and the Rockies: A Bibliography of Original Narratives of Travel and Adventure 1800-1865* (Columbus, Ohio, 1953); Thomas D. Clark, *Travels in the Old South*, 3 vols. (Norman, Okla., 1956-1959).

[20] Walter Blair, *Native American Humor (1800-1900)* (New York, 1937), p. 27, n. 1.

While the celebrated travel books of Frederick Law Olmsted deal primarily with the economics and sociology of the ante-bellum plantation, they incidentally describe the folk religion of the slaves, whose shouting, singing, dancing, and exhorting bred traditional forms of song, music, dance, and sermon. The *American Diaries* listed and described by William Matthews offer another type of writing, akin in some ways to travel literature.[21] A close examination will repay the student of folk custom and folk speech. Indian captivities represent a bridge for the passage of Indian supernatural beliefs and myths, in garbled form, into white culture.[22]

A library folklorist may not only scan separately the news-paper, periodical, chapbook, broadside, jestbook, almanac, diary, or travel book, but he can investigate all these sources concurrently on a regional basis. In *Jonathan Draws the Long Bow*, the author relied on such printed materials for a picture of New England legends and humorous folktales in the first three centuries of American history. The town history proved to be a particularly rich repository of local legends. In his *Tall Tales of Arkansaw*, James R. Masterson surveyed the printed folk humor of one state from a miscellany of writings, coming up with a meaty spread that serves as an excellent complement to the field collections of Vance Randolph from the Ozarks. One social historian, Thomas D. Clark, had the sagacity to observe, "There is no richer source for the study of human activities on the frontier than its thousands of humorous stories."[23] From the *Spirit of the Times*, the reminiscences of preachers and travelers, Kentucky newspapers, and even pub-lished statutes he constructed *The Rampaging Frontier*, which illustrates folkways in the backwoods society of the trans-Allegheny West.

[21] *American Diaries, An Annotated Bibliography of American Diaries Written Prior to the Year 1861*, compiled by William Matthews (Berkeley, 1945).

[22] See "The Indians' Captives Relate Their Adventures" in Vail, *The Voice of the Old Frontier*, pp. 23-61; and Howard H. Peckham, *Captured by Indians: True Tales of Pioneer Survivors* (New Brunswick, N. J., 1954).

[23] Thomas D. Clark, *The Rampaging Frontier* (Indianapolis and New York, 1939), p. xii.

When Clark describes the traditional games on the frontier, such as throwing shoulder stones and long bullets, or gander-pulling and dog-fighting, he provides fresh materials and valuable datings for the comparative folklorist, who must depend on the printed accounts of eyewitnesses in the backwoods for information about now vanished pastimes and recreations. The student of games will find special rewards in the accounts of frontier sports and pleasures, from shooting matches to corn huskings, assembled by R. Carlyle Buley from Indiana, Illinois, and Michigan newspapers, travel books, and pioneer recollections.[24] Arthur Palmer Hudson prepared his anthology *Humor of the Old Deep South* from the printed resources of Alabama, Louisiana, and Mississippi. No anthologies have yet appeared which take for their objective the recovery of the full range of identifiable folklore—songs, tales, proverbs, beliefs, customs, speech—from the printed resources of a state or region. Some attempts have been made, however, to trace the legend of the regional character symbolizing the folkways of the state. Masterson has suggested the legendary outlines of the Arkansawyer, Leach of the Texan, and Moore of the Kentuckian:[25] what of the Missouri puke, the down-Easter from Maine, the Georgia cracker, the Ohio Buckeye, the Illinois Sucker, the Indiana Hoosier?

Printed sources capture oral traditions only by accident, and must always rank below field collections. Today the folklorist deliberately seeks out these traditions with notebook and tape recorder; yet collectors in the United States have barely tapped the immense resources of oral folklore. A few regions are relatively well collected—the Spanish Southwest for instance —while others, like New England, have been virtually ignored.

[24] R. Carlyle Buley, *The Old Northwest, Pioneer Period 1815-1840* (Indianapolis, 1950), vol. I, pp. 315-36.
[25] James R. Masterson, *Tall Tales of Arkansaw* (Boston, 1943); Joseph Leach, *The Typical Texan* (Dallas, 1952); Arthur K. Moore, *The Frontier Mind* (Lexington, Ky., 1957).

Here I shall suggest three lines of fieldwork which would attempt to explore systematically the oral wealth of the American heritage.

In order to achieve representative samplings of folk tradition which will permit cross-regional comparisons, a series of planned and coordinated field trips is necessary in place of the casual and haphazard collecting that is now the practice. One approach to the task of selecting regions for intensive collecting can be made by following the guidelines already available in the relic areas of folk speech mapped by fieldworkers on the Linguistic Atlas of America. This Atlas, directed by Hans Kurath, with the assistance of the late Marcus L. Hansen, was designed to plot the historical movements of American population, but has unfortunately suspended operations after mapping speech areas of eastern United States. After discussions with Kurath, who suggested that the eastern seaboard had been unduly neglected by folklore collectors fleeing to the mountains during summer vacation, this author, in July, 1956, essayed a pilot field trip to Jonesport, high on the coast of Maine, to determine whether such a relic area would prove rich in other types of folklore besides folk speech. Seventeen days in the field yielded over three hundred tales and songs from twenty-two of these Yankee lobstermen, who had clearly preserved a vigorous folk tradition of maritime lore, local anecdote and rhyme, and supernatural legend.[26] For comparative purposes, similar trips should explore relic areas all along the coast: Essex County and Cape Ann in Massachusetts; the Narragansett Bay area of Rhode Island; Long Island Sound; the Delamarvia peninsula lying between Chesapeake and Delaware Bays; Albemarle Sound in North Carolina; and the coastal strip from Cape Fear to the mouth of the Peedee River in South Carolina. The results of comparable quests in these zones would inform us whether or not these relic areas are indeed reservoirs of folk tradition, and if the nature of these traditions alters markedly with the regions. Inland relic areas

[26] A sample of the collection is given in "Collecting Folklore in Jonesport, Maine," *Proceedings of the American Philosophical Society*, CI (1957), 270-89.

can also be tested, although beyond the Appalachians these have not yet been fully mapped.

Collecting possibilities on an ethnic basis are so over-whelming that one scarcely knows where to begin. The great collections of nationality folklore in the United States all belong to the future. Only one book-length study exists, *South Italian Folkways in Europe and America,* by Phyllis Williams, pub-lished in 1938 by a sociologist wishing to prepare a handbook for social workers dealing with Italian immigrants. Her case studies are chiefly drawn from New Haven. Just to illustrate the potentialities in this type of tradition: in one day's record-ing with a Greek-American family in northern Michigan the writer obtained some twelve thousand words of excellent texts on a variety of legendary themes, involving saints, demons, heroes and possessors of the evil eye.[27]

One can only wildly surmise what is collectable from a Greek-American population of 180,000 families, and how the acculturation process may differ among Greeks who stayed in the Boston area, opened restaurants in the Midwest, or formed a sponge-fishing community in Tarpon Springs, Florida. Dorothy Lee has already shown the possibilities of differentiat-ing Greek immigrant lore according to geographical areas of emigration.[28] What holds for the Greeks will apply of course to the whole spectrum of nationality traditions. We have been tantalized with articles on Czech songs in Nebraska, Portuguese folklore in New Bedford, Basque tales in Oregon, Armenian stories from Detroit, Chinese customs in San Francisco[29]—but

[27] "Tales of a Greek-American Family on Tape," *Fabula,* I (1957), 114-43.

[28] Dorothy Demetracopoulou Lee, "Folklore of the Greeks in America," *Folk-Lore,* XLVII (1936), 294-310.

[29] See the references in my notes to ch. IV, "Immigrant Folklore," in *American Folklore* (Chicago, 1959), pp. 295-96, and such other references as Jon Lee, "Some Chinese Customs and Beliefs in California," *California Folklore Quarterly,* I (1942), 337-57; C. Merton Babcock, "Czech Songs in Nebraska," *Western Folklore,* VIII (1949), 320-27; Susie Hoogasian and Emelyn E. Gardner, "Armenian Folktales from Detroit," *Journal of American Folklore,* LVII (1944), 161-80; Stanley L. Robe, "Basque Tales from Eastern Oregon," *Western Folklore,* XII (1953), 153-57; Leah R. Yoffie, "Yiddish Proverbs, Sayings, etc., in St. Louis, Mo.," *Journal of American Folklore,* XXXIII (1920), 134-65.

in place of a ten-page article we would like to see a ten-volume collection.

One ethnic group has indeed seen the wish come true. The Lithuanian collections made by Jonas Balys in the United States demonstrate the rewards attainable by the skilled collector with the knowledge of the Old Country language and culture. Most of the publications covered in the eighteen Library of Congress cards of his writings on this subject are in Lithuanian, but translated texts or notes are available in his articles on "Fifty Lithuanian Riddles" and "Lithuanian Ghost Stories from Pittsburgh," his Folkways recording of "Lithuanian Folk Songs in the United States," and his volume *Lithuanian Folksongs in America,* which contains 472 song texts and 250 melodies.[30]

More than mere collecting is involved in the gathering of immigrant folk traditions, for all kinds of acculturation studies are possible in the vast laboratory of the United States population. We can compare the early mid-nineteenth century Irish immigrants with the latest Puerto Rican influx; we can contrast Italians in the city with Italians in the countryside, Sicilians with north Italians, Red Finns with anti-Red Finns, Issei with Nisei Japanese, the Jews of Brooklyn with the Jews of Los Angeles, the Scandinavian with the Slav, the European with the Asiatic. From such rural-urban, cross-regional, cross-generational and cross-ethnic studies we can learn much about the social life of immigrant groups and their compromises with American civilization. Also we can obtain texts and customs of European folklore now obsolescent in the Old Country. In developing a collecting program among nationality pockets, the International Institutes and ethnic organizations in all large northern cities would prove immediately helpful.

[30] Balys describes his techniques for making contacts among Lithuanian immigrants—through ethnic newspapers, priests, ethnic clubs—in *Four Symposia on Folklore,* pp. 74-78. "Fifty Lithuanian Riddles" was published in the *Journal of American Folklore,* LXIII (1950), 325-27, and "Lithuanian Ghost Stories from Pittsburgh" in *Midwest Folklore,* II (1952), 47-52. *Lithuanian Folksongs in America* is published by Lithuanian Encyclopedia Publishers, Boston, 1959.

A third large area for collecting folklore in the United States comes under the head of occupational lore. Men working together in a common trade or under one factory roof develop the cohesiveness, and the esoteric traditions, of an in-group. In the early days of folksong collecting, the song repertoires of cowboys and lumberjacks were revealed as surprisingly extensive hoards, but other aspects of their lore were slighted. It remained for a newspaperman, George Korson, to penetrate the grim and forbidding company towns of Pennsylvania coal miners, and dredge up hidden veins of balladry, legend, union lore, and craft traditions.[31] No comparable collections of occupational lore have yet been published, but a rich cache of material in the Indiana University Folklore Archives bears witness to the mass of folk tradition to be found in army barracks. Eighty-five folders hold texts of jinxes and hoaxes, bawdy ballads and song parodies, war tales descended from earlier wars, goldbricking yarns, atrocity legends, folktales of lucky escapes and unlucky fatalities, devoutly believed superstitions, glossaries of special terms, cycles about swashbuckling officers and offbeat GI's.

We can postulate similar categories of tradition for other modern American occupational groups—railroaders, truck and taxicab drivers, the crews of passenger liners and freighters; factory workers and labor union members; professionals in show business and sports; journalists; workers in specialized trades, like printing, whose customs Thorstein Veblen referred to in the *Theory of the Leisure Class;* and office workers of the white-collar world. Salesmen are the Yankee peddlers of today, glib of tongue, carriers of tales as well as of goods. In the public relations culture of twentieth-century America, everybody must be a storyteller, from the college president to the political campaigner. Nor are the older outdoor occupations

---

[31] George Korson, *Minstrels of the Mine Patch, Songs and Ballads of the Anthracite Industry,* and *Coal Dust on the Fiddle, Songs and Stories of the Bituminous Industry* (Philadelphia, 1938 and 1943); *Black Rock, Mining Folklore of the Pennsylvania Dutch* (Baltimore, 1960); and "Songs and Ballads of the Anthracite Miners," Record Album 16, issued from the Collections of the Archive of American Folk Song, Library of Congress.

once so productive of lore now all vanished; there are still quarry workers, shrimp and lobster fishermen, migratory fruit pickers, Erie canallers.

We have spoken about research opportunities in the library and in the field, but another large area, the folk museum, invites attention. Here the contrast with European accomplishments is most glaring, for systematic presentation of the material objects in folk culture dates back only about a decade and a half in the United States. Yet in this time some notable publications, richly and handsomely illustrated, have depicted existing collections of folk art. They include Jean Lipman's *American Folk Art in Wood, Metal and Stone* (1948), Erwin O. Christensen's *The Index of American Design* (1950), and *The Abby Aldrich Rockefeller Folk Art Collection* (1957). Although the definition of folk art is even more tenuous than that of folklore, it applies broadly to objects painted, hewn, carved, chiseled, woven, spun, and decorated by nonprofessional craftsmen and artists in a traditional manner. In the seventeenth, eighteenth, and nineteenth centuries, before the advent of mass-produced factory goods, traditional crafts and folk arts flourished in the city as well as on the farm.

The first problem of the American folklorist concerned with this subject is to locate and rescue examples of folk art for preservation and exhibit in the folklore museum. While the collector of songs and tales enters the living room seeking to record members of the family, the collector of pottery and quilts searches the attic, the basement, and the barn. In the future a single folklorist may engage in both these quests simultaneously.

Collecting for the folk museum promises indeed to rival the collecting of oral traditions. Only one American folklorist has so far ventured deeply into the folk museum sphere—Louis C. Jones, director of the New York State Historical Association. The Association's properties at Cooperstown include the Farmers' Museum, which displays farm and village buildings of frontier times, and the American Folk Art collection housed in the Fenimore House.[32] One example related by Dr. Jones may suggest the abundance of physical items obtainable by the enterprising searcher. In 1950 the authority on American primitive paintings, Nina Fletcher Little, asked Jones if there were houses in central New York with wall paintings or stencilings. He knew offhand of only one, in Ithaca, and its stenciled scenes had long been covered with wall paper. But upon initiating a hunt, he discovered within ten miles of Cooperstown itself a tavern covered from floor to ceiling with free-painted landscapes, and eventually he located half a dozen buildings within a twenty-mile radius of Cooperstown with extensive stencilings on their walls. The tavern was transported bodily to the Farmers' Museum, and the other wall paintings were acquired for the Folk Art collection.[33]

In a culture rich in home crafts, like that of the Pennsylvania Dutch, the folk arts extend to the kitchen utensils, the household furniture, the daily costume, the carriages, the tombstones, the barns. Here the question arises as to how far folk art in the United States encompasses folk architecture. The Pennsylvania German barns, decorated with traditional designs, clearly reflect the distinctive culture of their builders.[34] In most regions the data is still meager, but Austin Fife has acquired an impressive collection of colored slides of wooden fences, gateposts, and hay derricks in the Rocky Mountain states, and can illustrate their patterns of regional design.[35] José E. Espinosa published in 1960 an extensive monograph on the *santos*, or

[32] Louis C. Jones, "The Cooperstown Complex," *Antiques*, LXXV (February, 1959), 168-69. The William J. Gunn collection of over 600 American primitive paintings, acquired by Fenimore House, is described in Agnes Halsey Jones and Louis C. Jones, "New-Found Folk Art of the Young Republic," *New York History*, XLI (April, 1960), 117-231.

[33] Personal letter from Louis C. Jones, dated 16 October 1959.

[34] Charles H. Dorbusch, *Pennsylvania German Barns*. With introduction and descriptive text by John K. Heyl (Allentown, Pa., Pennsylvania German Folklore Society Yearbook, vol. 21, 1958).

[35] See "Hay Derricks of the Great Basin and Upper Snake River Valley" by Austin E. Fife and James M. Fife, in *Western Folklore* (1948), 228-39.

family images of patron saints, an indigenous expression of religious folk art in the Spanish southwest.[36]

As these artifacts of regional folk cultures are gathered in folk museums, the American folklorist will need to ponder their relationship to the oral forms he has studied in the past. Dov Noy, the director of the Ethnological Museum in Haifa, Israel, has actually traced magic amulets and rings to their possessors from allusions in folktales.[37]

Giant tasks face the collector of folk materials on several fronts, and their fulfillment can produce scholarly monuments, worthy of a place alongside the ballads of Child, the customs of Frazer, the motifs of Thompson, the riddles of Taylor. But the accumulation of texts and objects is not an end in itself. The documents and artifacts will offer data for broader and deeper syntheses within American cultural history. The historian of American life has steadily expanded his concerns to include literature, the fine arts, science, religion, and indeed all the manifold aspects of a civilization. He has made gestures toward folklore, and we can see the rewards in such seminal works as Theodore Blegen's *Grass Roots History* (1947), calling for historical treatment of the folk, and the studies of American cultural myths by Dixon Wecter in *The Hero in America* (1941), Henry Nash Smith in *Virgin Land* (1950), and Arthur K. Moore in *The Frontier Mind* (1957).

Yet in no area of American culture is the historian so misinformed as in folklore. The standard bibliographies in *The Literary History of the United States* and *A Guide to the Study of the United States of America* cannot fully be trusted.[38]

[36] *Saints in the Valleys. Christian Sacred Images in the History, Life and Folk Art of Spanish New Mexico* (Albuquerque, 1960).

[37] Dov Noy, "Archiving and Presenting Folk-Literature in an Ethnological Museum" (to be published in the *Journal of American Folklore*).

[38] For example, such works as Stanley D. Newton, *Paul Bunyan of the Great Lakes;* Frank Shay, *Here's Audacity! American Legendary Heroes!;* and Walter Blair, *Tall Tale America,* lack any validity as specimens of folk tradition (*Literary History of the United States,* ed. Robert Spiller et al., vol. III, Bibliography, New York, 1948, pp. 200, 203, 205). The unscholarly "treasuries" of American folklore by B. A. Botkin are recommended in D. H. Mugridge and Blanche P. McCrum, *A Guide to the Study of the United States of America* (Washington, D. C., 1960), pp. 785-98.

Because the pursuit of folklore in this country is riddled with so many amateurs, from writers of children's books to urbanized folk singers, the scholar in other fields frequently takes the wrong turn when he enters the maze of folk tradition.

For the future we can look toward an increasingly profitable synthesis between American history and folklore. Scholars in the two fields are gradually moving toward common ground, where all kinds of inviting research topics suggest themselves: the feed-in and feed-back between folk and popular culture; the folk stereotypes of politicians and the rituals of political behavior; the role of Old Country tradition in the life of the immigrant; the history of occultism in America; the development of regional identities and regional myths; the transition from supernaturalism to science in early American thought. As folklore study in America approaches maturity, its prospects for fresh and original explorations in the years immediately ahead appear exciting and adventurous.

MIDDLEWESTERN REGIONAL LITERATURE

JOHN T. FLANAGAN

O NE PARADOX of American literary history is that despite the persistent efforts of dedicated scholars for the past quarter of a century, so much remains to be done. Definitive biographies of many of our chief writers are yet to be written. Collected editions supplied with the necessary critical apparatus need to be published. The correspondence of major and minor figures should be brought together or at least transcribed from extant manuscripts and printed. It is surely extraordinary that, up to the present moment, Sidney Lanier is the only American author who has been given an adequate critical edition.

We have, to be sure, excellent biographies of certain important writers: for example, Carl Van Doren's life of Franklin, Ralph L. Rusk's life of Emerson, Gay W. Allen's life of Whitman, Arthur H. Quinn's life of Poe. But despite the spate of books devoted to Mark Twain there is still no satisfactory complete biography, and there is no comprehensive biography of Cooper or Simms or Hawthorne. The five volumes of Simms correspondence, the two volumes of Poe letters, and the six volumes of Emerson correspondence represent in handsome format the chief epistolary activities of these writers, although a good many letters by both Poe and Emerson have turned up since the editors supposedly finished their work. But we have no collection at all of the letters of Hawthorne or Howells, and the published letters of Mark Twain, Henry Adams, and Henry James appear in a multitude of places. Editions of the work of major authors are likewise disappointing. The Centenary Edition of Emerson and the subsequently published journals are excellent, but even these twenty-two volumes leave a fair amount of Emerson material uncollected. The New York Edition of Henry James does not even include all of James's fiction and is now out of print. Editions of Mark Twain omit almost as much Twain material as they include. There is no collected edition of the works of Howells, Simms, or Cooper.

Fortunately the picture also has many bright aspects. The multi-volume edition of the works and letters of Thomas Jefferson is one of the memorable publishing events of our century and, although still incomplete, has already proved a model for similar enterprises. A comparable edition of the writings of Benjamin Franklin will certainly prove to be of equal magnitude and utility. A scholarly edition of Melville's correspondence has just been published, and admirable attempts have been made to print the creative work of Melville in a uniform edition with elaborate introductions and annotations. But so far only five volumes have appeared and completion of the project seems somewhat remote. Thoughtful recent biographies of Howells, G. W. Cable, Henry James, and Henry Adams testify to the assiduity of capable modern scholars, and special studies of Poe, Emily Dickinson, and Stephen Crane have been revealing and provocative.

Up to this point I have been primarily concerned with the national scene and have chosen my examples chiefly from the East and the South. I should like now to turn to the Middle West and assess the situation in terms of the present.[1]

---

[1] A few years ago I attempted a similar survey of the field: "Some Projects in Midwest Cultural History," *Indiana Magazine of History,* XLVII (September, 1951), 241-50.

Some years ago Ralph Leslie Rusk published an invaluable book, dealing with the territory north and west of the Ohio River, which he called *The Literature of the Middle Western Frontier*. Here in two thick volumes he covered quite successfully all facets of literary activity up to his arbitrarily chosen terminal point. Unhappily for us today this date was 1840. For the hundred and twenty years that have elapsed since 1840 there is nothing of comparable extent. As a matter of fact, after years of working in similar territory, I should like to suggest that there cannot be. Rusk's method, if sedulously applied to the literary material produced in the Middle West since 1840, would exhaust any one man's industry and ability and almost any publisher's budget. The proliferation of writing in all fields that Rusk considered—literary, historical, journalistic, scientific, theological, educational—is so vast that it cannot be reduced to a single study. It must be divided, fragmented, broken up into subjects for special consideration, treated in monographs or carefully focussed dissertations.

It is gratifying to recall that in recent years really competent work has been done in the field of middlewestern literary and intellectual history. Merle Curti in the eleventh chapter of his monumental *Growth of American Thought* has supplied a fascinating synthesis of early intellectual trends and crosscurrents. Biographies of Timothy Flint, James Hall, Edward Eggleston, Vachel Lindsay, F. Scott Fitzgerald, and Theodore Dreiser do exist.[2] The autobiographical volumes of Harriet Monroe, Floyd Dell, Eunice Tietjens, and Edgar Lee Masters tell us much about the so-called robin's egg renaissance which took place in Chicago in the second decade of the twentieth century.[3] Monographs deal with the publishing house of Stone

[2] The chief examples: J. E. Kirkpatrick, *Timothy Flint* (Cleveland, 1911); John T. Flanagan, *James Hall, Literary Pioneer of the Ohio Valley* (Minneapolis, 1941); William P. Randel, *Edward Eggleston* (New York, 1946); Edgar Lee Masters, *Vachel Lindsay, A Poet in America* (New York & London, 1935); Arthur Mizener, *The Far Side of Paradise* (Boston, 1951); Robert H. Elias, *Theodore Dreiser: Apostle of Nature* (New York, 1949).

[3] Harriet Monroe, *A Poet's Life* (New York, 1938); Floyd Dell, *Homecoming* (New York, 1933); Eunice Tietjens, *The World at My Shoulder* (New York, 1938); Edgar Lee Masters, *Across Spoon River* (New York, 1936).

and Kimball, with *The Prairie Schooner*, with early theatrical activities in Chicago and St. Louis.[4] The *Mississippi Valley Historical Review* and the journals of the various middle-western historical societies have been consistently hospitable to articles dealing with the culture and literature of the region. Important articles, indeed, swell every annual bibliography. But still the tasks remain.

Consider, for example, Henry Rowe Schoolcraft, geologist, explorer, amateur ethnologist, agent to the Chippewa at Sault Ste. Marie and Mackinac Island. Partly because of his official position and partly because of his marriage to the grand-daughter of a well known Chippewa chief, he became interested in Indian legends and tales, and his collection of such materials in *Algic Researches*, 1839, made possible Longfellow's *Song of Hiawatha*. Yet there is no adequate study of School-craft. Many similar examples might be mentioned. Caleb Atwater, an Ohio lawyer and antiquarian who worked diligently for public education, and John Mason Peck, an energetic Baptist minister and editor in early Illinois, need modern evaluations. Ignatius Donnelly, novelist, pamphleteer, and stormy petrel of Minnesota Populism, has never received satisfactory treatment. Henry H. Sibley, a writer of competence besides being a soldier and the first governor of Minnesota, has been neglected. Peter Cartwright, the memorable Methodist circuit rider who once defeated Abraham Lincoln in a campaign for the Illinois legislature, has not been given a scholarly biography; and of William Henry Milburn, evangelist and social historian, there is no study at all. Among minor figures, Joseph M. Field, actor and sketch writer in pre-Civil War St. Louis, William D. Gallagher, Cincinnati editor and poet, Sol Smith, actor and theatrical impresario, and Maurice Thompson, Indiana poet and novelist, have virtually eluded biographers. Alphonso Wetmore, early St. Louis play-

---

[4] Sidney Kramer, *A History of Stone and Kimball . . . 1893-1905* (Chicago, 1940); Paul R. Stewart, *The Prairie Schooner Story* (Lincoln, 1955); W. G. B. Carson, *The Theatre on the Frontier* (Chicago, 1932) and *Managers in Distress* (St. Louis, 1949).

wright and litterateur, needs attention. There is no bio-graphical and critical study of Mary Hartwell Catherwood, once a greatly admired novelist of the old French settlements of the Great Lakes area, nor of Alice French, long famous under the pseudonym of Octave Thanet. In particular, the obscurity into which the name of William Marion Reedy has fallen seems strange. Reedy, for two decades the editor of *Reedy's Mirror* in St. Louis, was a master of invective and was especially devastating in his comments on national po-litical conventions. In diatribe not even H. L. Mencken a generation later was his superior. He was also notable for his encouragement of younger writers, and it should not be forgot-ten that the first epitaphs of the *Spoon River Anthology* (con-tributed by Edgar Lee Masters under the pseudonym of Webster Ford) appeared on the pages of his *Mirror*. But Reedy himself seems to have escaped attention.[5]

When the record is brought down to date, the omissions become even more glaring. Hamlin Garland died in 1940, Edgar Lee Masters in 1950, Sinclair Lewis in 1951. Twenty years after Garland's death the first biography appeared, and although it is satisfactory as a narrative of Garland's life it makes little attempt at literary assessment.[6] There is no biography of Masters or of Lewis. The only consequential study of Vachel Lindsay was written by Masters in 1935 and remains valuable because of the personal intimacy between the two Illinois poets. A recent biography, based on the now acces-sible cache of Lindsay material formerly housed in a Spring-field, Illinois, warehouse, sheds fresh light on Lindsay's life and

[5] Important periodical articles have of course been written about some of these figures. For example, Francis P. Weisenburger, "Caleb Atwater: Pioneer Politician and Historian," *Ohio Historical Quarterly*, LXVIII (January, 1959); Robert Price, "Mrs. Catherwood's Early Experiments with Critical Realism," *American Literature*, XVII (May, 1945), 140-51; John T. Flanagan, "Reedy of the Mirror," *Missouri Historical Review*, XLIII (January, 1949), 128-44. My comments refer only to published books. There are unpublished doctoral dissertations about Sibley (Minnesota, Wisconsin), Donnelly (Minnesota), Mrs. Catherwood (Ohio State), Reedy (Vanderbilt).

[6] Jean Holloway, *Hamlin Garland, A Biography* (Austin, 1960).

personality but is critically negligible.[7] A sound interpretation of Lindsay utilizing all the material now available is badly needed. Studies of writers who have recently passed from the scene, such as Lew Sarett, Phil Stong, Ruth Suckow, and particularly Louis Bromfield, have yet to appear. Also sounder books than those already published about George Ade and Eugene Field need to be written. An evaluation of James Whitcomb Riley not so much as a writer but as a cultural phenomenon would seem almost imperative.

Definitive books on living writers are, of course, impossible, and the attempt to produce such studies might be unwise. Yet the celebrity and assured position of certain writers present a challenge that might well be taken up. Floyd Dell, particularly in his early period as literary editor, feminist, and novelist, deserves attention. As a young critic in Chicago he had much to do with the careers of such aspiring writers as Sherwood Anderson. John G. Neihardt, the first poet to write an epic on the settlement of the Missouri Valley and the author of several valuable biographical volumes, merits more attention than he has heretofore received. An assessment of the work of the prolific August Derleth, active in the fields of fiction, verse, and expository prose, will eventually need to be made. And the increasing stature of Wright Morris, already the author of a dozen books, many of which focus on the fictional town of Lone Tree, Nebraska, will require critical evaluation. Most conspicuously lacking, perhaps, is any full length study, biographical or critical, of the work of Carl Sandburg. It will be a formidable task indeed to estimate objectively the writings of so versatile and productive a man, not to speak of tracing chronologically the career of one who has been in the public eye for almost half a century as poet, troubador, biographer, novelist, and historian. Moreover, it will be difficult to supplement Sandburg's own autobiographical

[7] Eleanor Ruggles, *The West-Going Heart, A Life of Vachel Lindsay* (New York, 1960).

volume, *Always the Young Strangers*. But surely the task cannot be deferred much longer.

One interesting facet of the cultural development of the Middle West has been the rise of certain small towns as literary or intellectual centers. Such a community was Jacksonville, Illinois, after the Civil War, when Dr. Hiram K. Jones organized the Plato Club and subsequently the American Akademe there, and also founded a journal devoted to idealistic philosophy. Such too were Crawfordsville, Indiana, in the 1880's the home of Lew Wallace, Meredith Nicholson, and Maurice Thompson; and Davenport, Iowa, around the turn of the century when Alice French and George Cram Cook were residents, and young Floyd Dell was experimenting with verse, prose, and Socialism. The full history of these communities has never been written, nor has the cultural life of the cities of the Middle West, with the possible exception of Chicago, been fully recorded.

Although occasional articles on theatrical or literary activity have appeared in periodicals, much else has been neglected, such as the writing of poetry and fiction, the founding of the almost innumerable literary magazines, the organization of lyceums and discussion groups, the inception of publishing firms, and the establishment of libraries. In an earlier day Cincinnati and St. Louis were in turn the cultural centers of the Middle West; later Chicago began its dominance at the center of what Frederick Jackson Turner called an imperial domain. But other cities had their cultural influence too— Indianapolis, Detroit, Des Moines, Minneapolis, St. Paul; and their stories remain for the most part unchronicled.

The magazines in particular need historians, for they provided not only media for local contributors but often genuine literary stimulation. One of these journals was the *Lakeside Monthly*, which Francis Fisher Browne edited in Chicago both before and after the great fire of 1871. Another was the *Bellman*, which William C. Edgar kept lively and solvent for thirteen years in Minneapolis. The Des Moines *Midland Monthly Magazine,* the Iowa City *Midland* edited by John T. Frederick, and *Reedy's Mirror* in St. Louis must also be mentioned; as well as such older periodicals as the *Illinois Monthly Magazine,* published at Vandalia from 1830 to 1832, the *Western Monthly Magazine* of Cincinnati, and the *Hesperian* of Columbus and Cincinnati. Certainly a full-length study of the Chicago *Dial,* 1880-1916, the most important conservative book-reviewing journal in the country before its transference to New York City as an avant-garde publication, is long overdue. The function of these various journals was unique. At their most imitative moments they slavishly followed eastern models; certainly Browne had the *Atlantic Monthly* in mind when he planned his *Lakeside Monthly.* But all of them strove to develop a western point of view, to call attention to trends and events of peculiar regional interest, and to encourage local writers while at the same time preserving certain standards. Like the publishing houses which strove to maintain a list of writers of belles lettres before their best authors were siphoned off by New York firms, they often fought a losing fight, but their collective impact was significant.

The reference to publishing, indeed, suggests an important corollary. Readers, students, and teachers of middlewestern literature have alike been disturbed by the frequent unavailability of certain notable books; these books, allowed to go out of print earlier, have become increasingly important today as cultural documents and in some cases have even taken on greater aesthetic value than was ascribed to them when they were first published. Some commercial houses, such as the Minneapolis firm of Ross and Haines, and certain university presses, such as the University of Oklahoma Press (especially notable for its handsome and astonishingly low-priced Western Frontier Library), have been commendably active in restoring important regional books to print. Many such editions, unfortunately, are issued in facsimile form in order to hold down the costs and are not provided with the necessary critical introductions and annotation.[8]

There is a real need for the republication of many early books in scholarly editions. The novels of Timothy Flint, for example, are seldom found in any one library and are prohibitively priced in the rare book market. In particular, *Francis Berrian*, the first American novel to be given a partial setting in Mexico, should be reprinted. Moreover, Flint's autobiography, *Recollections of the Last Ten Years*, one of the most valuable documents we have of early life in the Ohio Valley, deserves a reissue. The important early stories of James Hall, certainly among the better tales of the first half of the nineteenth century, have never been collected. J. L. McConnel's *Western Characters* would be much better known if readers did not have to search so hard for the original and only edition of 1853. The best novels of Edward Eggleston have been frequently reprinted, but there is no collected edition, and the earlier books are often elusive. Eugene Field's first and most amusing book (if we disregard the newspaper drawings with captions entitled *The Tribune Primer*) was *Culture's Garland*. It had only one edition, 1887, although some of its material reappeared in later volumes. I should even like to suggest the desirability of making once more available John W. Monette's *History of the Discovery and Settlement of the Valley of the Mississippi*, which to J. Christian Bay was "the best general descriptive history of American culture and progress in the middle West."[9] Published in 1846, it has been superseded by more reliable and complete histories, but it retains interest and appeal. Indeed the ambitious publisher might well survey with a critical eye the 400 titles itemized by Dr. Bay in his three "handfuls" of western books and choose one or more to reissue. The result might be something like a gamble on the stock market with

[8] The reprint of Mrs. Frances Trollope's *Domestic Manners of the Americans,* edited and introduced by Donald Smalley (New York, 1949), is a notable exception.

[9] J. Christian Bay, *A Second Handful of Western Books* (Cedar Rapids, 1936), 41.

the additional benefit that many readers and collectors would gain by the speculation.

There are other projects demanding attention, to some of which Hamlin Garland pointed as long ago as 1894.[10] One of the great commercial activities of the Middle West has been lumbering, and Michigan, Wisconsin, and Minnesota are still thought of as the lumbering states, although the focus of the industry has long since shifted westward. Only the most valiant efforts of Chambers of Commerce have succeeded in localizing Paul Bunyan in the northern Minnesota communities of Brainerd and Bemidji. The impact of lumbering on letters has never been assessed. Surely a literary synthesis is needed which would treat in one work the genuine logging-camp ballads collected by Franz Rickaby, the woods-inspired poetry of Douglas Malloch and Lew Sarett, along with the romances and tales of Stewart Edward White, Eugene Thwing, and Edna Ferber.

Again, the importance of rivers in the life of the Middle West from the days of the voyageurs to the invention of the steel barge deserves literary examination. Mark Twain has preserved once and for all the flavor of the steamboat era in his *Life on the Mississippi,* and such volumes as Joseph Mills Hanson's *Conquest of the Missouri* and Charles Edward Russell's *A-Rafting on the Mississipp',* good as they are, can only be considered as runners-up to Twain's classic. But Edna Ferber's *Show Boat* and Richard Bissell's *A Stretch on the River* suggest other aspects of river life and point to a vast fluvial and marine literature which needs its own investigation and classification.[11]

Mining too, whether the object be coal, copper, lead, or silver, has long been a subject of cultural as well as economic interest. Mining activities have centered in northern Michigan, southwestern Wisconsin and northwestern Illinois, south central

[10] Hamlin Garland, *Crumbling Idols* (Chicago, 1894), 14-15.
[11] Books about nine middlewestern streams are included in the Rivers of America series, but so far the Miami, Chippewa, Minnesota, St. Croix, Des Moines, and Platte rivers have gone unrecorded.

Missouri, and, of course, the Cuyuna, Vermilion, and Mesabi ranges of Minnesota. From these probings into the soil have come minerals enough to sustain American industry for generations, but also books. Miners, like lumberjacks, sailors, and stevedores, sing or tell tales. Their songs and stories have not only been written down but have also provided material for writers as different as Phil Stong, Skulda Banér, and John D. Voelker (the Michigan supreme court justice who under the pseudonym of Robert Travers wrote the highly successful *Anatomy of a Murder*, 1958). Mining as a literary theme would certainly repay study.

Another profitable kind of investigation concerns certain character types. The schoolmaster has interested writers from Queen Elizabeth's tutor, Roger Ascham, who in 1570 wrote a tract called *The Scholemaster*, to Washington Irving, who immortalized the Yankee pedant in his portrait of Ichabod Crane. The backwoods teacher was long a favorite character of the middlewestern writer. J. L. McConnel described him in *Western Characters*, Caroline Kirkland depicted him on the Michigan frontier, and Joseph Kirkland introduced a New England schoolmistress into his novel of early Illinois, *Zury: The Meanest Man in Spring County*. Most famous of all the rural teachers, of course, is the hero of Edward Eggleston's *The Hoosier Schoolmaster*, who eventually bested the neighborhood rowdies and won the respect of his pupils. Subsequently Sinclair Lewis painted satirical portraits of the pedagogue in such novels as *The Trail of the Hawk* and *Gideon Planish*. In the earlier novels the schoolmaster was generally the district teacher boarding around, a kind of harmless drudge who often gave singing lessons as well as instruction in the three r's. In more recent fiction he may be the impecunious college professor or the dangerous free-thinking radical, for American society has consistently undervalued the professional educator. Yet one cannot forget Willa Cather's quiet, sensitive portrait of the scholar given to historical research, Professor St. Peter, who adds so much to the charm of her novel *The Professor's House*.

To the schoolmaster might be added the middlewestern clergyman and the middlewestern businessman, made fictionally notorious by Sinclair Lewis in *Elmer Gantry* and *Babbitt* but by no means limited to them. The evangelist, missionary, and pastor have appeared often in middlewestern fiction from Eggleston's novel, *The Circuit Rider,* to the excellent stories written about the Catholic clergy by J. F. Powers. Big business with a Chicago background has been the theme of Will Payne in *The Money Captain,* of Theodore Dreiser in *The Titan,* of Frank Norris in *The Pit,* and of Robert Herrick in *The Memoirs of an American Citizen.* Indeed, the church sometimes becomes big business, in both literature and reality. The changes in the conception of the minister and the merchant, their increasingly larger orbits and their growing impact on the community as revealed in life and as imaginatively reflected in literature, are worth special consideration.

This is perhaps also the place to mention the need for a reassessment of the role of the immigrant in middlewestern literature. In the pioneer period the immigrant in his own right was relatively unimportant since all settlers were immigrants, and barriers of language, religion, or race were less significant than the need to offer a united front against such common foes as hostile Indians and wild beasts. Moreover, at that time the immigrants from across the Atlantic were numerically insignificant. But by the time of the Civil War conditions had changed and the problems of immigrants had become special. Eventually these problems found their reflection in literature, and novelists began to focus attention on such figures of the immigrant world as the fugitive, the opportunist, the adventurer, the timorous, and the conscience-stricken. Foreign writers like Johan Bojer and Vilhelm Moberg have chosen these figures for protagonists of novels about North Dakota and Minnesota.[12] Conrad Richter's trilogy of settlement

---

[12] Johan Bojer, *The Emigrants,* 1925; Vilhelm Moberg, *The Emigrants,* 1951, *Unto a Good Land,* 1954, and *The Last Letter Home,* 1961. The original Swedish titles of Moberg's first two novels are rather revealing: *Utvandrarna* (The Outwanderers) and *Invandrarna* (The Inwanderers).

in southeastern Ohio represents one conception of the home-
steader's life; his characters come from a Pennsylvania Scotch-
Irish family who live a nomadic existence until finally the trees
are felled and the game killed off.[13] Another conception of the
transplaced settler is revealed in James Farrell's picture of the
Chicago Irish, who retain many of their traditional mores in
their painful adjustment to the life of an American metropolis.
If Farrell's Studs Lonigan is a sensational example of failure to
make the adaptation, other characters like Danny O'Neill
succeed.

Far different is the role of the immigrant in the fiction of
O. E. Rölvaag or Willa Cather, where fishermen and artisans
from the old world became prairie farmers and sought to adapt
themselves to a new means of livelihood as well as to a new
society. If the first generation, as represented by Rölvaag's
Per Hansa and Miss Cather's old Shimerda, often failed, the
second generation inevitably triumphed. The polyglot character of most of the prairie states is sufficient proof of the final
assimilation. Since immigrants from Norway, Sweden, Holland,
Germany, Finland, Ireland, and Czechoslovakia filled in the
open lands of the Middle West, it is only natural to find them
appearing in the literature about these lands, whether written
by foreign-born novelists like Martha Ostenso and S. K.
Winther or by native middlewesterners like Hamlin Garland,
Herbert Quick, and Feike Feikema.[14] The complex portrait
of the immigrant in middlewestern fiction especially calls for
sharper definition and analysis. Some of this literature, incidentally, written in German or Norwegian or Danish, has never
found a translator. Novelists whose work remains largely
untranslated include Heinrich Balduin Möllhausen, Waldemar
Ager, Johannes B. Wist, and Enok Mortenson.

[13] Conrad Richter, *The Trees*, 1940; *The Fields*, 1946; *The Town*, 1950.
[14] For example, Martha Ostenso, *Wild Geese*, 1925; S. K. Winther's trilogy
about Danish pioneers in Nebraska, *Take All to Nebraska*, 1936, *Mortgage Your
Heart*, 1937, *This Passion Never Dies*, 1938; Hamlin Garland, *Main-Travelled
Roads*, 1891; Herbert Quick, *Vandemark's Folly*, 1922; Feike Feikema (later
known as Frederick Manfred), *This Is the Year*, 1946.

With a literature linked as closely to the soil as most literature of the Middle West has been, it would be strange indeed if writers ignored the beliefs, the idioms, and the traditions of the folk. And of course they have not done so. Remove from Mark Twain, if this could be done, his frontier tall tales, the Negro superstitions, the numerous backwoods cures and proverbs, the rural locutions, the riverman's traditions, and his work would collapse. Mark Twain's obligations to folklore have long been apparent. But in other middlewestern writers the folk legacy is almost as important, though it has seldom been pointed out and indeed not always understood. Joseph Kirkland's novel *Zury* is a treasury of folk speech. Vachel Lindsay not only wrote poetry about folk heroes like Johnny Appleseed, but in his portraits of Lincoln and Andrew Jackson he contributed to the process of accretion by which historical figures become living legends. Moreover, his rhythms owe a good deal to the spiritual, the evangelist's hymn, the ballad, and the cakewalk. Songs and beliefs are scattered throughout the work of Hamlin Garland and reveal clearly the spirit of his "prairie folks," while if folk themes are less conspicuous in the novels of Herbert Krause, Willa Cather, and Sherwood Anderson, they often assume functional significance. Carl Sandburg is perhaps the best contemporary example of the writer who uses folklore creatively. His poems are redolent of folk speech, and his fiction, his autobiography, even sections of his life of Lincoln are imbued with tradition and popular lore. Surely there is no more memorable collection of the folk speech of America than Sandburg's *The People, Yes*. The artistic use of folklore by these writers and many others is a particularly challenging subject.

One other topic, it seems to me, awaits the middlewestern literary or cultural historian, and here I wish to suggest interdisciplinary study. Some of our best regional writing has been particularly faithful to the physical background, almost photographic in its description indeed, and (what is even more important) authentic in its interpretation of the milieu.

In the same way, some of the most effective landscape painting
has been the inspired work of native artists who, usually after
foreign training, returned to their earlier environment to make
a record on canvas. It would be an interesting study to
correlate story and landscape, the fictional figures and the
characters of the painting; to show, in other words, how one
art complements and reinforces the other, thus presenting a
more vital and indelible impression. Certain pairs intrude
themselves at once upon the imagination. The river canvases
of George Caleb Bingham and the steamboat and raft scenes
of Mark Twain are but two faces of the same coin. Ruth
Suckow and Grant Wood portray the same angular Iowa characters, the same gaunt faces and uncompromising attitudes.
It is true that Wood's bulbous trees and rounded cornfields do
not recur in Miss Suckow's descriptions of farm scenes; but the
opulence of the artist's dinner for threshers finds many an
analogy in the novelist's pictures of family meals. The immense
open spaces of Nebraska and Kansas, both wheat and cattle
states, find sympathetic interpreters in Willa Cather and John
Steuart Curry. The line storms and lurid skies of the painter
have parallels in the prairie scenes of *My Ántonia* and *O
Pioneers!;* and the simple, outdoor life of the settlers, the
primitive religion, the sensuous contact with the land, seem
characteristic of both craftsmen. Sinclair Lewis is not notable
for rural description, yet in *Main Street* and elsewhere there is
an appreciation of the grain fields, the richness of the crops,
even the vigor and color of the autumn that one finds so vivid
in the paintings of Adolph Dehn (born, like Lewis, in a Minnesota prairie community). Perhaps it is not stretching the
point too far to suggest that a study of the Chicago paintings
of Aaron Bohrod, with their lonely elevated stations, tilting
lampposts, dilapidated houses, and dirty street corners might
go hand in hand with a reading of the disturbed career of
Farrell's Studs Lonigan, who spent his days and especially his
nights in equally dismal surroundings. In all of these cases the
painter and the novelist have chosen identical themes and

details, even identical dramatic contrasts, and a comparison of the two interpretations would not only enrich each but would reveal the sensitivity and salience of artistic visions that differ only in intensity.

Many other possibilities present themselves for profitable investigation. Ardent Populists like Hamlin Garland and Herbert Quick need to be placed in their proper tradition, and the decline of the Populist ideal might well be followed through the milder Socialism of Carl Sandburg. The literary influence of so seminal a social thinker as Thorstein Veblen should be considered despite the thorny awkwardness of Veblen's own style. The organic theories of Frank Lloyd Wright in the field of architecture might well be applied to other arts, and the merits of Wright as an author should certainly be considered. The middlewestern autobiography (and here one thinks of Floyd Dell, Harriet Monroe, Clarence Darrow, Howells, Sandburg, Twain, Dreiser, Augustus Thomas, Edgar Lee Masters) sometimes seems a particularly clear reflection of the individualism and independence for which the entire region has been noted.

Thoreau, in a famous essay, remarked that in his daily walk of three or four hours he usually sauntered in a westerly direction, since he equated the West with the ideas of freedom and wildness. Middlewesterners of the twentieth century, prone to consider themselves free from the cramping ideology of isolationism, like to claim both sophistication and deep concern with the world's affairs. But as one of the younger sections of a relatively young nation we have many problems still before us, many jobs to do and a wide area in which to do them. Happily we labor under no restrictions beyond those of individual competence. Our tasks are not imposed by the State or censored by a Politbureau. To us Siberia is not a symbol of incarceration, but still a geographical province. As Archibald Macleish once said symbolically, "America is West and the wind blowing."

THE BOOKTRADE
AND PUBLISHING HISTORY

DAVID KASER

RANKLIN D. Roosevelt once said that there were few
businesses so intimately interwoven with the national
fabric as a publishing house. He was speaking at the
time of the house of Harper, the important firm which
both influenced and was influenced by almost every important
cultural movement and economic development in our country
in the last century and a half. Founded in 1817, it was already
strong enough to survive the closing of the banks fifteen years
later and the panic twenty years later, when many of its less
sturdy competitors were bankrupted. With its massive organization for distribution, it pumped its many publications, school
books, novels, religious books, classics, learned treatises, into
the country's hinterlands and vanishing frontiers, enlightening,
entertaining, educating, and influencing its citizens. Almost
singlehanded, about 1840 Harper wrested the unofficial headquarters of the publishing industry away from Philadelphia
and Boston and established it in New York, where it has
remained to this day. It was active and vocal in its early
opposition to international copyright and was in the vanguard
of every major publishing development from 1830 to 1900.

It is ironic that a scholarly history of this publishing house has not yet been written. Although it is ironic, it is not unusual, because serious, book-length histories of the many aspects of the American booktrade are well-nigh nonexistent. This is true despite the fact that, if a bibliography of the American booktrade existed, it would be encumbered with a great number of entries, because there has been much writing on the subject. Yet very little of this writing has shown the kind of thoroughness and dispassion that characterize reports of scholarly investigations.

Most of the entries which would appear in a bibliography of the American booktrade would fall into one of three groups. First, there would be the personal essays of dilettante enthusiasts. Second, there would be the histories of publishing firms which had either undertaken or commissioned such publications. Third, there would be the memoirs and reminiscences of individuals who spent their lives in association with the trade. None of these is necessarily reliable as history.

This is not to deny the utility of these many books—especially the ones in the two latter categories—for some of them are veritable mines of useful information. One of the best company histories, for example, is *The House of Harper*. The author is Joseph Henry Harper, whose position in the firm and the family enabled him to present a unique and interesting view of the firm's development, but even the kindest critic could not ignore the book's bias.[1] Furthermore, since such volumes are usually written for publicity purposes, accuracy is of secondary importance, and they are consequently often plagued with error, and, as anyone acquainted with publishers' opinions of footnoting would guess, they almost invariably omit documentation.

The memoirs and reminiscences written by persons who have spent their lives in the publishing or bookselling industries are especially informative, but these writings are not scholarly

---

[1] Joseph Henry Harper, *The House of Harper; a Century of Publishing in Franklin Square* (New York, 1912).

studies. As primary sources, however, they furnish useful kinds of raw material out of which historical studies can be made. A fair number of such volumes exist, but perhaps not as many as one would expect. Booksellers and publishers are, after all, a literate lot and might be expected to write more about their business than they have done. Many, of course, have written prolifically about things other than publishing. James Redpath is an example, as are both Mathew and Henry C. Carey, as well as Samuel G. Goodrich. Mathew Carey and Goodrich also wrote their autobiographies—the former dull, the latter fascinating—recounting many anecdotes and details of the nineteenth-century booktrade which would otherwise have been lost to us, as is true also of James C. Derby's life-story.[2]

What then remains to be done in the American booktrade? There remains serious, scholarly, documented, and dispassionate investigation and reporting of almost all aspects of the American booktrade—of author-publisher relations, of the economics of authorship, publishing, and bookselling, of the mechanics of book distribution and marketing, both wholesale and retail, of the impact of the bookstore on the culture and economy of the community, of the complex internal workings of the trade, of the aesthetics of book and type design, illustration, and binding, of the techniques of printing, paper manufacture, and bookbinding, of the development of the publisher from the printer-bookseller, of Anglo-American booktrade relations, of governmental impact on the trade, of unionism in the trade, of the rise of copyright, and of many other subjects. The rest of this paper will discuss several specific research opportunities lying in this list. Most of these suggestions will be from the nineteenth century, not because all of the good opportunities exist there, but rather because space limitations prevent discussion of all periods and because the nineteenth

    [2] Mathew Carey, "Letters," in *New England Magazine*, July, 1833-Dec., 1834; Samuel G. Goodrich, *Recollections of a Lifetime, or Things I Have Seen in a Series of Familiar Letters to a Friend, Historical, Biographical, Anecdotal, and Descriptive* (New York, 1857); James C. Derby, *Fifty Years among Authors, Books and Publishers* (New York, 1884).

century is even less well studied than the eighteenth and the twentieth centuries.

A glance at Besterman's bibliography of bibliographies[3] might easily give the impression that there is nothing under the sun about which someone has not compiled a list of books. This may be almost true; yet, surprisingly enough, bibliographers seem to have devoted very little attention to one phase of their profession, since a thorough list of references to published sources on the American booktrade does not exist. There are many partial lists to be sure, selected lists, lists restricted by period or by place, or by some other delimitation, but a comprehensive, retrospective bibliography of the booktrade has not yet been compiled. This task would seem to demand early attention from someone interested in the field, because its accomplishment would facilitate future scholarship, obviate unnecessary duplication of effort, and point up areas of needed research. It would not need to be annotated, although annotations are always useful; it should be classified by some logical arrangement; and it should be well indexed. Current annual bibliographies of the subject have been published in recent years by several agencies, and there have been several efforts through published and manuscript lists, to "bibliographize" the business, but a definite compilation has not yet been made.

Work needs to be done on another kind of bibliography; but this task is one of great magnitude and will no doubt require the efforts of a society of scholars rather than of an individual. The editor of the *Antiquarian Bookman* recently labeled as "a national disgrace" the fact that no list has been compiled of books published in America between 1800 and 1820.[4] The issues of American presses during the seventeenth and eighteenth centuries are quite well detailed in Evans' *American Bibliography,* and those since 1876 are documented in the

[3] Theodore Besterman, *World Bibliography of Bibliographies* (Geneva, 1955-1956).

[4] Sol Malkin, "The Golden Age of Bibliography," in *Antiquarian Bookman,* 18 (Dec. 15, 1956), 2228.

American Catalogue and its successors.[5] A preliminary check-list of books published in the United States between 1801 and 1820, compiled by Shaw and Shoemaker, is now appearing. Although it is drawn entirely from secondary sources and repeats their errors as well as adding its own, it is widely hailed by bookmen. There has been no previous attempt to cover these two decades. The period from 1820 to 1871 has been poorly done by the nineteenth-century booksellers Orville Roorbach and James Kelly, and it requires early redoing.[6] Several years ago I had occasion to spotcheck Roorbach's reliability and found that, of a group of 732 titles known to have been published, only 442 or 60 percent are listed in Roorbach. Of this number, fully 320 entries, or 72 percent, either omit some essential detail or state some such detail incorrectly. Surely this hiatus in our national trade bibliography should be filled as soon as possible.

The two bibliographical projects mentioned above would be of great utility in conducting almost all other kinds of investigations into the American booktrade. The former is necessary to enable us to learn what has already been examined; the latter is necessary because we cannot intelligently assess the contribution of a publishing house unless we know what books it has issued. A third kind of bibliography—one that could be compiled by an individual—would also soon prove its utility. It would be a guide to unpublished source materials in the booktrade. Some of these materials will no doubt come to light upon completion of the National Union Catalog of Manuscripts which is now under way. Others will be revealed by the projected guide to the manuscripts of American authors planned by the American Literature group of the Modern Language Association. Nonetheless, for the time being, caches of dusty material lie hidden in many libraries, attics, archives, and other

[5] Charles Evans, *American Bibliography* (New York, 1903-1959); *American Catalogue of Books, 1876-1910* (New York, 1941).

[6] Orville A. Roorbach, *Bibliotheca Americana, 1820-61* (New York, 1852-61), and James Kelly, *American Catalogue of Books Published in the United States from Jan. 1861 to Jan. 1871* (New York, 1866-71).

repositories throughout the country awaiting exploitation by industrious scholars, and unlikely to be examined until their existence is known. These materials are now usually located by scholars through a combination of fortuitous accidents, ingenious hunches, creative enterprise, some serendipity, and a great deal of searching, traveling, and corresponding. With good reason scholars will always wish to go over ground already trod, but surely the availability of a guide such as is here described would do much to overcome the present lack of human economy and would, as well, act as a spur to additional research.

A guide to source materials in the American booktrade would point, for example, to the large body of Ticknor & Fields papers now housed in the Baker Library at Harvard University. One important document from among these papers—the *Cost Books of Ticknor & Fields*—was edited and published by the Bibliographical Society of America a decade ago, and it has proved its value to American literary historians and bibliographers many times over. The cost books give complete production information, titles, authors, size of editions, payment to authors, cost of composition, press work, paper, and expenses, for each of the titles—over 1300—issued by Ticknor & Fields between 1832 and 1858. During the latter part of this period the firm, which is a forerunner of the Houghton Mifflin Company, was the most important general publisher in the country. Although a general history of this firm is now being prepared, this large corpus of unpublished material in the Baker Library can supply insight into many details of the nineteenth-century booktrade about which we know very little today.

Also preserved intact are several large segments of the papers of the Carey firms—forerunners of today's medical house of Lea & Febiger and the country's largest general publisher in the 1830s. Sections of this material, which is preserved at the Historical Society of Pennsylvania and the American Antiquarian Society, have been used by scholars, and this firm's cost book for the period 1825-1838 has been edited and is now in press, but other huge portions of it are practically untouched. We are much in need of a good, definitive biography of the founder of this firm, the irascible, lovable, cantankerous, generous, civic-minded, and astute business man, author, publisher, economist, and philanthropist, Mathew Carey, one of the authors whose manuscripts are being located by the MLA's Committee on Library Manuscript Holdings. This will make the preparation of his biography easier than it would have been in the past. A great man, and a friend to the small as well as the great, Carey came from Ireland in 1784 and settled in Philadelphia, where he died in 1839. His many contributions to his age and to posterity have not yet been satisfactorily examined.

Another collection of papers which are housed in the American Antiquarian Society are those of the Philadelphia publishing house of McCarty-Davis. To my knowledge no study of this firm has ever been made, though it published for a quarter of a century following its establishment in 1816. Still another very valuable collection of papers preserved at Worcester are those of the Boston firm of printer-publisher-booksellers, West, Richardson and Lord, founded in 1794 and lasting almost a century. "These papers include business correspondence, bills from printers, partnership papers, inventory records, copyright certificates, leases, as well as bills for presses and type."[7]

Other important papers have also found their way into institutions. Much of the correspondence of the Boston firm of Roberts Brothers reposes today in the Columbia University Libraries. An interesting history of this firm was recently prepared by Professor Raymond Kilgour and issued by the University of Michigan Press.[8] The literary records of the London house of Bentley are now in the University of Illinois. Although not an American firm, Bentley's extensive relations

---

[7] Rollo G. Silver, *The Boston Book Trade, 1800-1825* (New York, 1949), 9.
[8] Raymond Kilgour, *Messrs. Roberts Brothers* (Ann Arbor, 1952).

with American houses—for example, as Harper's London agent —enhance the value of this collection to students of the American trade.

Many publishing house records have been destroyed by accident, as in the case of Harper's disastrous fire in 1853; others have been pulped in ignorance of their research value. Still others remain in the hands of the original firms. Records which have been retained by firms are usually available for consultation by scholars, as has been attested in the prefaces and introductions to published studies. For example, Professor C. Harvey Gardiner acknowledges access to the company records of Little, Brown, of Lippincott, and of Harper, and expresses appreciation for their hospitality.[9] Yet few scholars appear to have recognized publishing house records as being good sources of information. Professor David Randall, in describing his twenty-two years with Charles Scribner's Sons, states that "it was rarely indeed in all the years I worked with that publishing firm that any scholar, author, or librarian working on a subject or an author we had published either recently or ninety years ago, inquired, 'Don't you have some material on this lad?' Occasionally Tinker would send someone down from Yale, or a bibliographer such as Jacob Blanck would appear to examine file copies and check points in our printed books—that was about all."[10] It is seldom necessary for an author to write into his introduction, as did the above-mentioned Professor Kilgour in one of his books, that a certain publisher "first denied the existence of any records and then refused completely to cooperate, not even bothering to answer letters. . . . Such an attitude is not at all characteristic of American publishers: other, and more important, firms with which I have had dealings have been most friendly."[11]

[9] C. Harvey Gardiner, *Prescott and His Publishers* (Carbondale, Ill., 1959), [vii].

[10] David Randall, "Institutional Collecting of Books and Manuscripts," *Proceedings of the Conference on Materials for Research in American Culture* (Austin, Texas, 1956), 14.

[11] Raymond Kilgour, *Estes and Lauriat; a History* (Ann Arbor, 1957), 7.

There are bodies of material of a different nature also awaiting examination by scholars. One of the largest batches of American bibliographic raw material is the vast collection of work slips gathered by the American Imprints Inventory under the W.P.A. It is now housed in the Union Catalog Division of the Library of Congress. These slips, one for each early American imprint located by the inventory, are gathered together by city, and within city by year, but have had little else done to them. They are unedited, uncollated, and almost unknown to scholars. Yet this collection is, to the person who would spend some time working with it, an enormous warehouse of crude information about the American booktrade. Occasionally a graduate student from Catholic University sorts out a segment of these slips, organizes them, and prepares a bibliographical essay concerning them for his masters thesis. An example is J. A. Donnelly's *Check-List of Maine Imprints from 1821 through 1825, with an Historical Introduction.* Huge quantities of these slips, however, remain untouched by scholars.

Another large corpus of material which remains essentially untapped but which is of great potential value to bibliographers is also preserved in the Library of Congress: the records of copyright filed between 1790 and 1870. Located in the Rare Book Division, these records fill about 615 volumes and are, of course, available for consultation by scholars. Their research value cannot better be described than by Martin A. Roberts, quondam chief assistant Librarian of Congress. "That these records [he states] contain a wealth of information fundamental to the bibliography of the United States needs no emphasis. . . . They are the basic sources for a history of our literary and typographical arts for the period which saw those arts spring from the swaddling clothes of the eighteenth century to the giant stature of the nineteenth. At a rough estimate these records may contain 150,000 entries. And this wealth of material is substantially untouched."[12]

[12] *Records in the Copyright Office Deposited by the District Courts Covering the Period 1790-1870* (Washington, D. C., 1939), 13.

Still other kinds of unpublished material concerning the American booktrade await consultation by the researcher. Surely a source of much valuable information is the Jackson E. Towne Collection of the History of Printing in America at Michigan State University. Comprised for the most part of the papers, notes, ana, and other documents of the indefatigable researcher Douglas C. McMurtrie, this collection is a veritable treasure trove of bibliographical information. Among other useful items in this collection are the galley proofs of the several unpublished volumes of McMurtrie's monumental *History of Printing in the United States*. Other similar collections of the unpublished ana of scholars are preserved elsewhere in the country. Some such notes repose in the Grolier Society. Much bibliographical data gathered by Dr. Wilberforce Eames lies unpublished in the New York Public Library. The American Antiquarian Society contains a collection of manuscript notes gathered by Melvin Lord toward a projected history of the Boston booktrade, 1686-1870.

Although very few histories have been written on individual publishing houses, even fewer studies have been conducted which examine separate aspects of the trade which cut across several or many publishing firms. Yet there are many "horizontal" studies which should be carried out. A good example of such a study is Dr. Frank Schick's useful book on the "paper back" in America, in which the author discusses the contributions to the paperback publishing industry of many nineteenth and twentieth-century houses.[13]

Comparative studies of the contributions of many publishers to other single aspects of the trade would also be welcome. There has thus far been little interest, for example, in American techniques of book-marketing, yet its important bearing on American cultural development would not be questioned. We know that many books before 1830 were sold by itinerant hawkers who peddled their wares from cabin to plantation, especially in the South and the Western Country, but with the

---

[13] Frank Schick, *The Paperbound Book in America* (New York, 1958).

exception of the colorful Parson Weems, we know little about the details of their operations, the prices they charged, the books they sold, or their impact on the community. We know also that vast numbers of books were marketed between 1824 and the Civil War through what were called Book Trade Sales, where representatives of the trade from the entire country gathered once or twice annually in Boston, New York, or Philadelphia, and bought unbound books in wholesale lots at auction. Two brief articles have been written about the Trade Sales, yet they continue to remain a "mystery of the trade" to scholars.[14] The process of book distribution known as "exchanging," wherein one printer-bookseller swapped products of his press, usually unbound, for the products of his neighbor's press, also remains a trade "mystery" today. Surely herein lie several interesting "horizontal" studies waiting to be pieced together.

Studies need also to be conducted into the problems and history of the publication of special kinds of books. Although some scholarly attention has been devoted to the publishing of school books, we are not yet quite aware of the enormous stimulus which they gave to the educational development of the country. Vast quantities of school books were sold in dry goods stores, in drug stores, print shops, and by wandering peddlers, in addition to regular bookstore outlets. Indeed, Noah Webster's blue-back *Speller* sold thirty-five million copies, and it is surpassed only by the Bible itself for the record as an all-time bestseller. Competition among publishers to get their school books "adopted" by local school boards sometimes became almost savage. Stern relates that "Saloon keepers in the West and Middle West often acted as members of local school boards, with obvious results, and one luckless publisher's representative, whose competitors had set a trap for him, was forced to flee a St. Louis 'adoption' in the dead of night minus

---

[14] W. S. Tryon, "Book Distribution in Mid-Nineteenth Century America"; David Kaser, "The Origin of the Book Trade Sales," *Papers of the Bibliographical Society of America*, 41 (1947), 210-30; 50 (1956), 296-302.

overcoat and shoes."[15] In spite of its inherent drama, the story of the publication of school books has not been finally written.

Another kind of horizontal examination which could be profitably conducted in the booktrade is a study of a publishing or printing family or dynasty. One of the best-known American printing families is, of course, the Bradfords—William, Andrew, James, Daniel, Thomas, Samuel, John, and others—who plied their trade in various locations east of the Mississippi. Their saga has been written, but there are other printing families which also deserve examination. There are, for example, the Usticks—Thomas and Stephen of Philadelphia, John S. of Knoxville, John G. of Lexington and Abingdon, Virginia, Thomas, Joseph, and William of St. Louis, and W. W. Ustick of La Crosse, Wisconsin—printers all. We should know more about this family, and about the Stewarts, the Halls, and the Clarks.

There are also many frontier printers whose activities should be examined in detail. These men followed closely behind the pioneers, carrying their presses and type cases on wagons and keel boats, setting up shop wherever they could be assured a list of 150 subscribers to their weekly newspapers. Theirs was a difficult lot. Their paper supply might fail to arrive from Pittsburgh before winter ice shut off river transportation, forcing them to close for the season. The mail carrier from Nashville might fail to arrive, so that there was no news for the weekly issue. A postmaster of a different political persuasion would "overlook" forwarding their newspapers to subscribers when they contained editorial matter with which he took exception. To be sure, there was always the problem of recalcitrant debtors among their subscribers and advertisers. The following anecdote, quoted from the Philadelphia *Saturday Courier* for December 21, 1833, is exaggerated, but the spirit is almost authentic: "We heard lately of a newspaper establishment in Indiana, somewhat novel in character. A printer has provided himself with a supply of wooden types, and having set up the form of his paper, each of his subscribers furnishes

15 Madeleine B. Stern, *Imprints on History* (Bloomington, Ind., 1956), 322.

him with a piece of linen or muslin of the proper size, where-upon the printer inks his type with swamp mud, and takes the impression upon the cloth for each patron, who receives his *paper* on Saturday, and after reading it, has the cloth washed and sent back in time for the next impression."

But the newspaper was only part of the work of the frontier printer. He kept a small stock of books—the latest Waverley and Cooper novels, inspirational literature, the *Union Primer*, an almanac, and a hymnal. He also printed and bound forms and blank books. He usually had a small book in press, a sermon, a Fourth of July oration, the minutes of a local Baptist conference, or, if he were lucky, he might also own the franchise for the territorial printing and would issue governmental docu-ments. He seemed always to be in need of "a new apprentice, preferably one from the country" as well as "a journeyman printer of steady habits. None other need apply." Vertical studies would be welcome of many of the pioneer printers.

In addition to studying individual printer-publishers, the publishing history of communities can be profitably examined. Some cities, of course, have had more illustrious booktrade histories than others. Cincinnati's publishing history has been written as an Ohio State University dissertation.[16] Similar examinations could be made of Detroit, Chicago, St. Louis, Nashville, New Orleans, and other cities. Cities also lend themselves well to another useful kind of compilation: making a directory of the local booktrade. Several have been published in recent years. An example is the Browns' *Directory of the Book Arts and Book Trade in Philadelphia to 1820* (New York, 1950). Others are available for New York, Boston, Baltimore, St. Louis, and Rhode Island. The frequency with which they are consulted by scholars in this field vouches for their utility. A different compilation which would be of considerable use would be a directory of printers' and publishers' imprints, but unfortunately none as yet exists.

[16] Walter E. Sutton, "Cincinnati as a Publishing and Book Trade Center, 1796-1880" (Unpublished Ph.D. dissertation, Ohio State University, 1947).

Special studies of a different nature would also prove fruitful and meaningful, such as studies of foreign-language publishing in certain geographical areas. Some work of this kind has already been done. The German-language press has been studied in Virginia, Missouri, Indiana, and elsewhere, but there are other languages and other locations. Another special subject deserving study is that of women in the booktrade. Lydia R. Bailey, printer of Philadelphia, turned out much creditable work during the three decades following her husband's death in 1807, yet we know very little about either the woman or her printing office. We know little of Mary Carroll, who came alone to this country from Ireland at the age of fourteen and sold books in New Orleans until she died in the cholera epidemic of 1833. Neither do we know anything of Eunice Coverly, bookseller of Boston, or of Mary Buglass, bookbinder and bookseller of Philadelphia. A paper of this kind, all too brief, was recently published.[17]

Many interesting and useful studies could be conducted on some of the techniques of printing. We do not yet know enough about type-founding in the United States, or about stereotyping. A brief paper has recently been published by J. E. Alden on "Scotch Type in Eighteenth Century America."[18] Surely there was also influence on American printing by Dutch letter-founders. A good book was brought out by the Harvard University Press in 1954 called *The Growth of the Book Jacket*, by Charles Rosner. Although not limited to the book jacket's use in this country, it contains much good information on American bibliography. Similar studies of other aspects of book production would be welcome: on the details of binding books in the olive boards typical of the early nineteenth century, on the rise of cloth binding in the 1820s and 1830s, and on early American craft binding. Professor Gardiner's book, mentioned above, could well stand as a model for future

---

[17] E. M. Parratt, "Women Printers and Engravers in San Francisco," *Bulletin of the New York Public Library*, 56 (1952), 43.
[18] *Studies in Bibliography III*, 270-74.

studies of author-publisher relations. We know little about the development of the modern publisher out of the eighteenth-century printer-bookseller. An examination should be conducted into the rise of the literary agent, the Negro press, the university press. All of the nineteenth-century booktrade journals should be analytically indexed. The University of Virginia issued a slender book in 1950 on *Jefferson's Ideas of a University Library,* which consisted of a series of letters from Jefferson to the Boston bookselling firm of Cummings, Hilliard and Co. Did not the booktrade have an impact upon the development of other American libraries as well?

These are only a few of the many and various research opportunities in the historical American booktrade. Many additional opportunities are described in Professor Rollo G. Silver's useful article on "Problems in Nineteenth-Century Bibliography."[19] The influence of the trade upon the culture of the country is obvious, yet it has attracted little scholarly attention. Topics are ripe to the plucking; fields are fallow to the researcher, and there remains much to be done.

[19] *Papers of the Bibliographical Society of America,* 35 (1941), 35-47.

POPULAR EDUCATION AND CULTURAL AGENCIES

DAVID MEAD

THE GENERAL problem of research in the area of cultural democracy is to provide adequate studies of the individuals and institutions involved in the promotion of popular education. Adequate studies will satisfy the expectations of modern scholarship by combining a thorough knowledge of the agencies themselves and an understanding of their social and intellectual environment. Scholars working in this field will be indebted to Merle Curti's *The Growth of American Thought* (New York, 1951) and to his other books and articles dealing with American intellectual history. He has given at least brief treatment to many of the research topics suggested here. The scholar will also find indispensable the numerous bibliographies of special subjects in our cultural history and the guides to the comments of foreign travelers.[1]

Perhaps no agency of popular education in our society has had more influence than the library, which from colonial times has furthered the dissemination of knowledge. Most library studies have dealt with famous book collections, reminiscences of early libraries or librarians, and discussions of such matters as library administration and organization. There have been relatively few modern histories of the library and its milieu as a significant part of our cultural growth. Jesse H. Shera examines the origins of the public library in New England from 1629 to 1855, and Sidney Ditzion discusses the social history of the public library in New England and the Middle States from 1850 to the end of the century.[2] Although both Shera and Ditzion rightly suggest that the growth of the public library in New England was similar to its growth elsewhere in the nation, the need remains for historical studies of the public library in the South and West. This is especially so because many public services of our libraries, particularly extension services, arose in the Middle West rather than in the East.

Much recent library research deals with technical problems, especially the development of automation or machine retrieval. Investigations of this kind have a special appeal nowadays because of their scientific nature and practicality. Another reason for the lack of interest in historical studies may be that most of the library science programs in American universities give scant attention to library history. But even in the technical area of library operation there are important historical studies to be made. The development of indexing services, emphasizing the work of William F. Poole, has not been adequately treated; nor has the development of classification systems, with special reference to the contributions of C. A. Cutter and Melvil Dewey.

A satisfactory history of state libraries, their origins, functions and relation to their regional environments, is still to be written. Histories of our major libraries, if they exist at all, are often either very old or are anniversary reminiscences which fre-

---

[1] J. Jeffery Auer, "American Public Address and American Studies: A Bibliography," *American Quarterly*, IX (Summer, 1957), 217-22; Clarence S. Brigham, *History and Bibliography of American Newspapers, 1690-1820* (Worcester, 1947); Winifred Gregory, *American Newspapers, 1821-1936* (New York, 1937); Jane Louise Mesick, *The English Traveller in America, 1785-1835* (New York, 1922); Max Berger, *The British Traveller in America, 1836-1860* (New York, 1943); Thomas D. Clark, ed., *Travels in the Old South,* 3 vols. (Norman, Okla., 1956-1959).

[2] Jesse H. Shera, *Foundations of the Public Library* (Chicago, 1949); Sidney Ditzion, *Arsenals of a Democratic Culture* (Chicago, 1947).

quently indulge more in sentiment than in scholarship. A recent exception is W. M. Whitehill's history of the Boston Public Library.[3] Among the many major American libraries that need the historian's attention are the Detroit Public Library, the Cleveland Public Library, the Enoch Pratt Free Library and the Peabody Institute Library in Baltimore. Moreover, the whole area of library extension service, such as branch libraries, county libraries, and even the modern bookmobile, being part of the movement to disseminate knowledge, deserves careful study.

There are several types of specialized libraries, such as mechanics' and apprentices' libraries, which receive only brief notice in most general histories of American libraries or of early education. Discussion is generally based on two articles, one by C. R. Aurner on mechanics' institutions and the other by Sidney Ditzion on mechanics' and mercantile libraries. A more recent treatment of these libraries, based chiefly on early newspaper accounts, as well as the annual reports and minutes of mechanics' institutes, is given in C. S. Thompson's study of the evolution of the American public library, 1653-1876.[4] The history of the mechanics' libraries needs detailed treatment, with emphasis on the social forces which fostered their growth and their ultimate decline. Useful bibliographies of research materials, including printed lectures given before the mechanics' societies, are provided by Thompson and by Sidney Jackson.[5] Files of nineteenth century newspapers as well as mechanics' magazines give additional information. Special topics which need research include the origins of the mechanics' library movement, the organization and operation of the

[3] Walter Muir Whitehill, *Boston Public Library: A Centennial History* (Cambridge, 1954).

[4] C. R. Aurner, "Mechanics' Institutions," *Iowa Journal of History and Politics,* XIX (July, 1921), 389-413; Sidney Ditzion, "Mechanics' and Mercantile Libraries," *Library Quarterly,* X (April, 1940), 192-219; C. Seymour Thompson, *Evolution of the American Public Library, 1653-1876* (Washington, 1952).

[5] Sidney Jackson, *America's Struggle for Free Schools: Social Tensions and Education in New England and New York, 1827-1842* (Washington, 1941).

mechanics' institutes, the work of William Wood, John Griscom, and Timothy Claxton in fostering early libraries, and the influence of the mechanics' institutes on the nineteenth century workingmen's movement and on the growth of popular education. Some of the larger mechanics' and apprentices' libraries deserve their own histories, for such histories of individual libraries as do exist are generally older and less satisfactory than John F. Lewis's *History of the Apprentices' Library of Philadelphia* (Philadelphia, 1924).

The mercantile library associations have received even less attention than the mechanics' institutes. They are briefly discussed in Ditzion's "Mechanics' and Mercantile Libraries" and in Thompson's *Evolution of the American Public Library.* Thompson gives a bibliography of primary and secondary sources relating to the mercantile libraries. The history of the mercantile libraries as part of the broad educational movement of the nineteenth century needs to be written. Abundant material is available for study, including records of mercantile societies, newspaper reports, and town and county histories. A considerable number of lectures given before the mercantile societies have been printed. Bibliographies of these are given in Thompson and Shera. *Hunt's Merchants' Magazine* and other commercial journals sometimes discussed affairs of the mercantile associations. Lists of early mercantile libraries, as well as mechanics' and apprentices' libraries, young men's associations, and athenaeums are given in a publication of the United States Bureau of Education on public libraries (1876).[6] This volume also contains a chapter on young men's mercantile libraries. A special topic for study is the influence of the mercantile library associations on the popular image of the American merchant and the mercantile profession. This image, which was often described by lecturers who addressed the mercantile societies, had great importance in our later social history. Some of the larger mercantile societies, such as the

[6] United States Bureau of Education, *Public Libraries in the United States of America, Their History, Condition, and Management* (Washington, 1876).

St. Louis Mercantile Library Association and the Cincinnati Young Men's Mercantile Library Association, were centers of social and intellectual life in their communities and should have separate histories.

There were many young men's associations which, unlike the mechanics' and mercantile societies, did not restrict their membership to a particular social class or vocation. These associations for mutual improvement have not been studied in detail. They are discussed briefly by Thompson, who again gives useful sources. Much information is available also in local histories and memoirs. A history of these organizations is needed, emphasizing their contribution to the nineteenth century popularization of knowledge.

In 1856 the educator Francis Lieber delivered a lecture before the Columbia (South Carolina) Athenaeum in which he complained that little information about the athenaeum was available.[7] His own lecture does not add much, and little has been written since about the athenaeum reading rooms and libraries. The Boston Athenaeum, which to foreign travelers was in a way a symbol of New England's intellectual prowess, received attention in a centennial publication of 1907, and there are a few other studies dealing with specific athenaeums.[8] Articles have been written about athenaeums in New York, Providence, and other cities. Bibliographies of these, and of lectures given before the athenaeums, are listed by Thompson. But the athenaeum movement and its contribution to cultural life have been somewhat neglected. Here, too, local histories should be combed, as some of them used manuscript records and reports no longer extant. Major athenaeums need their own histories, and older studies, including the history of the Boston Athenaeum, need to be redone.

[7] Francis Lieber, *The History and Uses of Athenaeums* (Columbia, 1856).

[8] *The Athenaeum Centenary: The Influence and History of the Boston Athenaeum from 1807 to 1907* (Boston, 1907); Joseph N. Ashton, *The Salem Athenaeum, 1810-1910* (Salem, 1917); Grace F. Leonard and W. Chesley Worthington, *The Providence Athenaeum, A Brief History, 1753-1939* (Providence, 1939).

During the period when early libraries were being established, a number of museums were founded in America. Research studies of natural science and historical museums have dealt mainly with technical matters such as historical restoration, dioramas, and preservation of specimens. Nearly every aspect of museum activity has received at least brief attention in L. V. Coleman's *The Museum in America*.[9] Notes on early museums and other agencies for the diffusion of scientific knowledge are given in Smallwood's *Natural History and the American Mind*.[10] This volume also contains useful bibliographies. Peale's Museum, which has attracted special attention, is discussed in several articles and in Sellers' *Charles Willson Peale*.[11] Brief studies of the historical growth of museums and their contributions to popular culture have been made by T. R. Adam and E. P. Alexander.[12] The familiar generalization that early museums were important to the popularization of knowledge conflicts with the equally familiar notion that early museums aimed at collection and scholarship, and that only the modern museum is important for education and interpretation. There is no authoritative history of natural science and historical museums which resolves this and other problems relating to the museum as a cultural force. Specific museums in our major historical societies are also worthy of study. Since museum records in the past were generally not well kept, reliance must be placed on newspapers, memoirs, local histories, and the like.

Museums were often operated by historical societies, which were established for various reasons, including the preservation of documents, encouragement of patriotism, and the dissemination of historical knowledge. Like other cultural agencies

[9] Laurence Vail Coleman, *The Museum in America*, 3 vols. (Washington, 1939).

[10] William M. Smallwood, *Natural History and the American Mind* (New York, 1941).

[11] Charles C. Sellers, *Charles Willson Peale*, 2 vols. (Hebron, Conn., 1939).

[12] T. R. Adam, *The Museum and Popular Culture* (New York, 1939); Edward P. Alexander, *The Museum, A Living Book of History* (Detroit, 1959).

which developed in the nineteenth century, the historical societies sometimes sponsored public lectures which popularized knowledge, even though the principal motive of the sponsors was usually to raise money. The nature of these societies and their contributions to American historical knowledge have been discussed by L. W. Dunlap, who notes that "The growth of American historical societies, like the development of most of our cultural institutions, has received little attention from students and scholars."[13] Historical societies still suffer from neglect, though progress has been made in such recent studies as those of R. W. G. Vail and of Paul Angle. Clifford Lord's history of the Wisconsin Historical Society is in preparation. Special activities and problems of modern historical societies are dealt with in the essays in memory of Herbert A. Kellar, recently edited by Hesseltine and McNeil.[14] The diversified aims and programs of the societies need further study, and their part in the dissemination of knowledge needs appraisal. City historical societies worthy of scholarly attention include those in Detroit, Rochester, Buffalo, and St. Joseph, Missouri. State historical societies and commissions which deserve study include those in Minnesota, Ohio, Pennsylvania, Massachusetts, Kansas, Missouri, Iowa, Nebraska, Montana, and Oregon. Research in these areas would undoubtedly be of much value to American historical societies generally by estimating their cultural achievement and their most productive organization and methods. The expansion of functions by historical societies during the past two decades has made special problems which, in the opinion of some historians, are more significant than discussion of the work of any individual agency. The impact of modern historical socie-

[13] Leslie W. Dunlap, *American Historical Societies, 1790-1860* (Madison, 1944), 220.

[14] R. W. G. Vail, *Knickerbocker Birthday, A Sesqui-Centennial History of the New York Historical Society, 1804-1954* (New York, 1954); Paul Angle, *The Chicago Historical Society, 1856-1954, An Unconventional Chronicle* (Chicago, 1956); William B. Hesseltine and Donald R. McNeil, eds., *In Support of Clio: Essays in Memory of Herbert A. Kellar* (Madison, 1958).

ties upon American life is a question of real importance, and the societies themselves recognize the need for extensive surveys and evaluations of their work.

The scholar who deals with the growth of popular education in America will find not only that the field of public address is of major importance to his study, but also that this field has not attracted much research concentration. Discussing the early nineteenth century, F. O. Matthiessen said in his *American Renaissance*: "In an age when the vogue of the modern newspaper had not yet quite begun and libraries were relatively scarce, public addresses were still a chief means of popular education: witness the rapid emergence of the Lyceum movement in the eighteen-thirties."[15] And J. Jeffery Auer remarks in his recent bibliography of public address and American studies that "authors of literary and intellectual histories have not as a rule given much prominence to the spoken word."[16] A start was made in Brigance and Hochmuth's work.[17] In general, however, scholars working in the field of oratory have concerned themselves with studies of rhetoric rather than with the spread of learning or other facets of cultural history.

Public address has been a significant educational medium for more than three centuries. Beginning in 1633, when John Cotton established the Boston Thursday Lecture, the public lectures given weekly in Boston and other New England towns became major social and intellectual events in the lives of the colonists. These lectures are briefly mentioned in New England political and church histories and in histories of American oratory, but they have not been studied thoroughly. The purpose, growth and decline of this early lecture system needs careful research. The importance of lecture day in Puritan social life needs special consideration, and the contributions of John Cotton, Cotton Mather and other clergymen to the lecture system should be assessed. Many of the Puritan lectures were

15 F. O. Matthiessen, *American Renaissance* (New York, 1941), 19.
16 Auer, p. 219.
17 William N. Brigance and Marie K. Hochmuth, *A History and Criticism of American Public Address,* 3 vols. (New York, 1943, 1955).

printed and are available for study. There are numerous references to the lectures in early town records and in the diaries of Samuel Sewall, Cotton Mather and John Winthrop. The Boston Lecture, which survived well into the nineteenth century, is briefly discussed by N. L. Frothingham and by Robert C. Waterston.[18] Nathaniel Hawthorne described the Puritan lecture day in a sketch called "Main Street."

There are numerous scholarly reports on the dissemination of political knowledge through oratory and pamphlets during the Revolutionary Era. Among them are books by Philip Davidson and by Alice M. Baldwin.[19] But much remains to be done in tracing the popularization of science in America before and after the war. While the activity of Franklin is well known, the efforts of Isaac Greenwood, Adam Spencer, Christopher Colles, William Claggett, Ebenezer Kinnersley and others deserve further study. In his public lectures Kinnersley introduced thousands of Americans to the wonders of science; at the time of his death in 1778 he was perhaps as well known as Franklin as an electrical experimenter. The lectures of early scientists in the colonial cities, especially Philadelphia, are noted by the Bridenbaughs.[20] Some of the postwar popularizers of science are discussed in books by John F. Fulton and Elizabeth H. Thomson, by C. R. Hall, and by Ethel M. McAllister.[21]

In the second quarter of the nineteenth century the lyceum became a major agency of popular education in America. The pioneer study of the lyceum movement is Cecil Branner Hayes' work, and the most recent treatment of the subject is by Carl

[18] N. L. Frothingham, *The Shade of the Past* (Boston, 1833); Robert C. Waterston, "The Thursday Lecture," *The Christian Examiner*, XXXVI (January, 1844), 24-37.

[19] Philip Davidson, *Propaganda and the American Revolution* (Chapel Hill, 1941); Alice M. Baldwin, *The New England Clergy and the American Revolution* (Durham, 1928).

[20] Carl Bridenbaugh, *Cities in Revolt: Urban Life in America, 1743-1776* (New York, 1955); Carl and Jessica Bridenbaugh, *Rebels and Gentlemen: Philadelphia in the Age of Franklin* (New York, 1942).

[21] John F. Fulton and Elizabeth H. Thomson, *Benjamin Silliman* (New York, 1947); Courtney R. Hall, *A Scientist in the Early Republic: Samuel Latham Mitchill, 1764-1831* (New York, 1934); Ethel M. McAllister, *Amos Eaton* (Philadelphia, 1941).

Bode.[22] Although there are a few articles and unpublished
theses dealing with the lyceum in particular cities or states, the
only published monograph relating regional lyceum history is
David Mead's, which is concerned with the Ohio lyceum movement from 1850 to 1870.[23] While lyceum growth in other states
was probably similar in many ways, the full meaning and
influence of the lyceum will not be known until thorough
studies are made of the institution's growth in other states.
Much is known of the lyceum in Massachusetts, but there is
no adequate history. Less is known of the lyceum in Connecticut, Vermont and the other New England states or cities.
There is little detailed treatment of the lecture system in New
York. The canal towns of that state were especially important
as lyceum centers because they were on a major lecture route
connecting the East and West. The western states have received less attention than they merit. There are articles about
the lyceum in Iowa and elsewhere, but no thorough accounts
of the institution in such important areas as Indiana, Illinois,
Minnesota, Michigan, Missouri, Wisconsin and Kansas. Except
in New Orleans, the lyceums in the cities or states of the South
have not been explored.

Nearly all of the available studies of the lyceum, or the
popular lecture movement as it came to be called, give up the
chase about 1860 or 1870. The lecture movement took some
new directions after the Civil War, but it did not lose its
energy. Under the influence of James Redpath and other
agents, the lecture system actually expanded. The developments of the late nineteenth and early twentieth century,
especially the relationships between the public platform and
the social unrest of the period, are important fields awaiting
research.

For scholars who prefer personality-centered studies, an

22 Cecil B. Hayes, *The American Lyceum, Its History and Contribution to
Education* (Washington, 1932); Carl Bode, *The American Lyceum, Town
Meeting of the Mind* (New York, 1956).

23 David Mead, *Yankee Eloquence in the Middle West* (East Lansing, Mich.,
1951).

inviting area for lyceum research lies in the platform experiences of American orators. There are so many published articles and notes about the lyceum appearances of Emerson that accounts of his lecture career require little more than collection and collation. But other important lecturers, such as Henry Ward Beecher, Wendell Phillips and Theodore Parker (whose manuscript lyceum diary has been preserved) have not been fully studied. Recent studies of important writers on the platform have been made by M. M. Sealts and by P. F. Fatout.[24] Still another approach to lyceum scholarship consists in the examination of professional groups, such as clergymen, scientists and editors, whose influence upon education in the nineteenth century was very extensive. Ministers represent the largest of these groups, and a study of their efforts to popularize learning through lectures would increase our knowledge of cultural history. Among the important clerical lecturers were William Ellery Channing, Henry Ward Beecher, Thomas Starr King, Thomas H. Stockton, F. H. Chapin and T. DeWitt Talmadge. The scholar will discover that, more often than not, these clergymen discussed general cultural subjects rather than religion on the lecture platform.

Another group of lecturers had considerable influence in forming literary taste in America by espousing the standards of the genteel tradition. They include Henry Giles, Edwin P. Whipple, George William Curtis, T. W. Higginson and Henry Norman Hudson. Giles, whom history has nearly forgotten, and Hudson popularized Shakespeare. Whipple, one of the most elegant essayists of the time and the American critic most respected by Nathaniel Hawthorne, has also been neglected by history.

The popularization of science was carried on by such eminent men as E. L. Youmans, Louis Agassiz, O. M. Mitchell and Benjamin Silliman, Sr. Their part in the spread of scientific knowledge needs study and appraisal, particularly during the

---

[24] Merton M. Sealts, *Melville as Lecturer* (Cambridge, 1957); Paul Fatout, *Mark Twain on the Lecture Circuit* (Bloomington, 1961).

1850's, when enthusiasm for science dominated the lecture programs of the nation. The science lecturer's most serious competition came from the travel lectures of Bayard Taylor, C. F. Hall, Isaac I. Hayes, P. B. Du Chaillu, George Kennan and others. A century ago, the travel lecturer fascinated Americans because he described places they could not visit; today he fascinates them because he describes places they can visit. The whole tradition of the travelogue, its famous lecturers, and its part in popular education are worth investigation.

Finally, the influence of nineteenth century newspaper editors in popularizing knowledge needs to be considered. Of particular interest are those editors who were known not only as city journalists and popular lecturers, but also as poets, novelists and essayists. This kind of literate and literary editor is somewhat less in evidence today, although the tradition of the small town editor, with his endless fund of local lore upon which he will lecture on any provocation, continues unabated. Among the prominent journalist-editors were the poet William D. Gallagher of the Louisville *Courier*, Theodore Tilton of the New York *Independent*, the poet George Prentice of the Louisville *Journal*, and the novelist and critic William T. Coggeshall, who edited newspapers in Cincinnati and elsewhere. The labors of such men, particularly those western editors who, by their own example, tried to stimulate a regional literature, should be further investigated.

We conclude with a few miscellaneous research topics in the general area of popular education. There are a number of endowed organizations, such as the Lowell Institute and the Cooper Institute, which have made conspicuous contributions to education. Many of them have their histories, but in some cases no history has been written; in others the work is old and needs to be redone with attention to the organization's influence on popular culture. A great deal of research has been done on early American schools, and some investigations have been made of important schoolmasters. Clifton Johnson's work on early schools and textbooks is now quite old, but the scholar will find in it numerous suggestions for research.[25] Further study is needed of American schoolbooks, emphasizing the ways in which they have been used to reflect American ideals and to provide a satisfactory image of the virtuous American. Useful contributions to this subject have been made by R. D. Mosier and John Nietz.[26] William McGuffey and Noah Webster have been the subjects of biographies. Other well-known educators who need thorough study are Josiah Holbrook, who founded the American lyceum, Henry Barnard and Horace Mann. All of these topics—and there are many left unnamed here—suggest the vast amount of research that needs to be done in the area of popular education and cultural agencies before all the necessary information will be available to provide a definitive account of intellectual democracy in America.

[25] Clifton Johnson, *Old-Time Schools and School-Books* (New York, 1904).
[26] Richard D. Mosier, *Making the American Mind: Social and Moral Ideas in the McGuffey Readers* (New York, 1947); John Nietz, *Old Textbooks* (Pittsburgh, 1961).

THE VISUAL ARTS
AND CULTURAL HISTORY

E. P. RICHARDSON

THE POINT I wish to contribute to the general discussion is that the field of studies in the visual arts is wide open, filled with opportunities to make great and useful contributions, whether on the level of small studies in detail or of wide, comprehensive views. Since time is limited and the field vast, I shall disregard the work already done in order to offer some suggestions of interesting and valuable work that awaits investigation.

Let me offer a few statistics based on personal experience. I brought out a history of American painting in 1956 in which I attempted to cover in one volume the entire story of painting in America since the discovery.[1] My publisher asked me to tell him how many American painters I mentioned by name. It surprised me to discover that I had mentioned 643 painters in the 450 years since the voyages of Columbus. In the bibliography of that book, however, I could only mention 64 of these artists to whom a modern monograph, biography, exhibition catalogue or some other reasonably respectable and accessible study had been devoted. In other words, one out of ten American painters is the subject of reasonably modern biographical studies. Yet painters are only the most conspicuous of those who practice the visual arts. If one turns to sculptors, engravers, silversmiths, cabinetmakers, cartoonists, all the varied talents that have given us our artistic heritage, the record is one of even more lamentable neglect. We need hundreds of biographical monographs and catalogues of individual artists and craftsmen to give us the basic documents for advancing study.

Let me offer two further sets of statistics. In the recent Groce-Wallace dictionary of American painters, sculptors and engravers before 1860,[2] there are, according to the publishers, more than 10,000 names. The Archives of American Art collects documentary material on all artists and craftsmen identifiable by name, in all fields of visual art, and upon the collectors, dealers, writers on art, and institutions that form the milieu in which the artists and craftsmen live. Its catalogue contains at the present moment 17,000 names.

Throughout history, sculpture has been considered a major art. The one serious attempt to write a history of sculpture in the United States was Lorado Taft's, published in 1903, with a supplementary chapter added in 1924.[3] Of the many sculptors included in Taft's book, it is difficult to discover one who is the subject of a good modern monograph.

If we turn to the field of graphic humor and satire, in which America has an interesting history ranging from the eighteenth century to the genial artists who work for *The New Yorker*, what good biographical monograph is there? Hardly more than the biography of Thomas Nast.[4] What has been written on the men who created the comic strip? Some of its inventors were men who later achieved international fame as serious

---

[1] Edgar P. Richardson, *Painting in America: the Story of 450 Years* (New York, 1956).

[2] George C. Groce and David H. Wallace, *Dictionary of Artists in America, 1564-1860* (New-York Historical Society, 1957).

[3] Lorado Taft, *The History of American Sculpture*, rev. ed. (New York, 1924).

[4] Albert Bigelow Paine, *Thomas Nast, his Period and his Pictures* (New York, 1904).

artists, like Lyonel Feininger; others were anonymous and retiring pixies like Herriman, the inventor of *Krazy Kat*. I consider this a contemporary folk art, whose creators have largely escaped attention.

I am a believer in the interest of popular material. I believe also in the value of local material in training students for original research. Art history in this country suffers from too great a dependence upon the photograph of a distant object which the student himself has never seen. Local material offers the student the discipline of working on original works of art, rather than on photographs which present experience at second hand. Local material requires the student to grapple with unanswered questions, large and small, in his own environment, rather than to work with secondary evidence and on material often already well explored.

American art historians have, on the whole, done solid work on some of the colonial craftsmen of New England, and progress has been made on the local arts and crafts in New York, Philadelphia, Baltimore and Charleston. Yet even for these areas there are few studies of individual craftsmen. The story of the arts and crafts of cities like Cincinnati, St. Louis, New Orleans, St. Paul, Chicago, Santa Fe, is still to be written. This is partly because of the prevailing focus of interest upon the highly skilled American handcrafts before 1830. The esthetic interest of the work of the skilled handcraftsman speaks for itself and has won an ardent following of collectors, antiquarians and popular writers. (The serious art history of the American craftsman still remains, largely, a work yet to be written.) The esthetic appeal of the machine-produced articles of the past century and a quarter is less widely felt: some people of taste would declare that it does not exist. The art historian has so far been reluctant to follow the sociologist and cultural anthropologist into the study of the effect of modern technology on the domestic arts. Yet the works of Lewis Mumford, Roger Burlingame, John Kouwenhoven, and Siegfried Giedion, have opened perspectives upon the nineteenth and twentieth century which are too suggestive to be ignored.[5] Deming Jarvis's mechanically-blown pressed glass (Sandwich glass) has become a collector's item and has found its way into art history. Other things surely will follow.

Our host at this conference, Mr. McDermott, has found material of extreme interest lying, unregarded, in the historical past of the Mississippi Valley, until he began work upon it. The careful research of Wilbur Peat, director of the John Herron Art Institute in Indianapolis, has resulted in a book on Indiana painters which is filled with new discoveries.[6] Museums have in general been ahead of the universities in forming interesting and significant collections of regional material, which still wait for the attention of the university art historian. As examples, let me mention only a few instances. Charles Nagel and Charles van Ravenswaay have brought together in St. Louis regional collections of arts and crafts of great importance. Perry Rathbone, while in St. Louis, did pioneer exploration in two great exhibitions, whose catalogues are full of material waiting for further studies.[7] Eugene Kingman has brought together in the Joslyn Memorial Gallery, Omaha, rich local collections, revealing the life of Nebraska and the Missouri Valley. In the Cincinnati Art Museum are fascinating collections of that city's artistic past. In Detroit we have two galleries of the arts of French Canada and early Detroit, illustrating the French colonial art of the St. Lawrence-Great Lakes waterway. The New York State Historical Association Museum and Farmers Museum at Cooperstown, New York, show how interesting the rustic arts of the nineteenth century can be. In New Mexico there is the Spanish-Mexican-

---

[5] Lewis Mumford, *Technics and Civilization* (New York, 1934); Roger Burlingame, *March of the Iron Men* (New York, 1938); *Engines of Democracy* (New York, 1940); *Backgrounds of Power* (New York, 1949); John A. Kouwenhoven, *Made in America* (New York, 1948); Siegfried Giedion, *Space, Time and Architecture, the Growth of a New Tradition* (Cambridge, Mass., 1941); *Mechanization Takes Command* (New York, 1948).

[6] Wilbur D. Peat, *Pioneer Painters of Indiana* (Indianapolis, 1954).

[7] Perry T. Rathbone, *Mississippi Panorama* (1949); *Westward the Way* (1954).

Indian tradition. All of these lie outside the more familiar areas of study, which are concentrated upon handcrafts of the Atlantic coast before 1830; each presents a hundred intellectual problems to those who will look at them.

A similar need for interpretation prevails in the field of architecture. The architectural historian of today is admirably free from snobbisms of period or place: remarkably good work is being done on nineteenth- and twentieth-century architecture. These studies, unfortunately, have not penetrated into the stream of American life sufficiently to stop, or even slow down, the daily massacre of American nineteenth-century buildings. Most of the cities of the Middle West, especially, seem bent upon throwing away whatever heritage of the past they may possess, in sheer ignorance of its meaning.

This leads me to the iconography of American cities and regions. What I. N. Phelps Stokes and John Kouwenhoven recently done for New York City;[8] what John F. McDermott has been working on for the Mississippi Valley, remain to be done for a great many American cities, whose history and architecture are part of our heritage. We wait for the iconographies of Boston, Philadelphia, Santa Fe, Salt Lake City, Cincinnati, Chicago, New Orleans.

Finally, the social, intellectual, and emotional milieu of the arts is a significant but almost untouched field. There are, first, the institutions of the arts (museums, art schools, art academies) some of which are among the great institutions of their kind in the world. It is surely significant that within the past century every city of any size in America has established an art museum. In the cities of the 10,000 to 100,000 class it generally takes the form of an art center, a building for activities rather than for collections of art, while in the larger cities it is a true museum of art. Large or small, these institutions

[8] I. N. Phelps Stokes and Daniel C. Haskell, *American Historic Prints, Early Views of American Cities, etc.* (New York, 1932) and I. N. Phelps Stokes, *New York Past and Present, its History and Landmarks, 1524-1939* (New York, 1939); John A. Kouwenhoven, *The Columbia Historical Portrait of New York* (New York, 1953).

represent an expression of the American people's respect for themselves and for their communities. The oldest is The Pennsylvania Academy of the Fine Arts in Philadelphia, founded in 1805, which is among the oldest existing institutions of art in the world. The story of these institutions is worth investigating. Who founded them and why? What was the history of each? Such topics would be very instructive.

In the Archives of American Art we are collecting the story of the art market and of art collecting. The records of art dealers, of auction sales, of collectors form essential elements in the history of taste and intellectual fashion. For instance, the earliest auction sale of art in this country was of the collection of a Swiss artist and naturalist, Pierre Jean du Simitière who died in Philadelphia in 1784. His collection was a curious mass of varied scientific and artistic collections. He was interested in the history, the artifacts and the language of the American Indians; he collected specimens of natural history and of geology; he painted portraits and made engravings, some of which are of historical value; he had a collection of coins and money. Du Simitière was the first of a great number of interesting, curious, often important, individuals who have been collectors of art.

What moves people to collect works of art? For some curious reason, those who do not collect are often unwilling to grant interesting or—still less—important motives to those who have this urge. Yet men of great personal stature, even statesmen like Washington and Jefferson or business leaders like J. P. Morgan and John D. Rockefeller, have been collectors of art. There is a strange popular notion that when a collector gives his collection to the public, as Andrew Mellon gave his to Washington, he is a philanthropist, but that when he is merely forming his collection, he is indulging in an idle vanity.

Yet what study is more interesting or more important for a historian than the deep-flowing tides of opinion and taste, often unconscious and always unpredictable, which shape each generation's view of the world? Let me mention a few of the phenomena of taste which raise questions for which we have no ready answers. What is the significance of the hunger for portraits in the early years of the Republic, a passion which gave place in the second half of the nineteenth century to an equal passion for landscapes? Why did the interest in human personality fade and an interest in the world of nature take its place? About 1875 came the rise of the esthetic movement, of which Whistler was the standardbearer. At the same moment that one current of taste preached Art for Art's Sake, there appeared a movement to revive the handcrafts, the arts of daily life which were being destroyed by the rise of factory production. The arts and crafts movement, beginning with the centennial of 1876, is another current of thought whose story has never been written.

About the same time there arose a great hunger for collecting art, resulting in the growth of art museums and private collections which have brought to this country, in the last seventy-five years, hundreds of thousands of works of art from every continent, every historical age, and every phase of human civilization. These social phenomena are of challenging interest. It would be well to broaden the field still further and to examine the arts as an index of civilization, not only from the point of view of the art historian, but calling in the historian, the sociologist, the cultural anthropologist, the critic, the archivist, to see what each of these can contribute to our understanding of the arts in America.

TASTES
IN RECREATION

PHILIP D. JORDAN

THE COMMON man's pleasures, from earliest times to the present, not only reflect a zest for living but also mirror rather faithfully mores and tastes. Man lives in an eye world and an act world. He derives amusement both from observation and from participation. At one moment, he watches drama on his television screen; at another he exerts himself with bowling, tennis, or golf. His relaxations vary according to his education, social position, income, and ambition. Some are simple and others sophisticated. Not too long ago, when history was preoccupied with politics, some historians failed to see the importance of cultural history. Even today there are those who may view with disdain the brightly lit stage upon which a nation's people sing and act and dance in their folkway and set to spinning an almost endless merry-go-round of festivals, games, hobbies, and bizarre amusements.

So large is the area of recreation that one can only begin to suggest specific topics, and always it must be remembered that each topic is part of a total social context. This is mentioned because sometimes the cultural historian is so preoccupied with description that he ignores interpretation.

Curiously enough, the theater, in its many aspects, although long the darling of the public, never has lured many historians to writing about it. Although much is recorded, need still exists for full accounts of the legitimate stage in such large urban communities as Washington, Atlanta, St. Louis, Minneapolis and St. Paul, and Seattle. Models exist in Kendall's study and in Odell's history of the New York stage, although the latter is more of a compendium than an integrated narrative.[1] Research could be rooted in dissertations and journal articles, and enriched by a deeper probing into sources not already tapped. Accounts are lacking of individual opera houses, of the efforts by local groups to bring live drama to their communities, of public reaction to plays. Indeed, histories of small-town theatrical events would be beneficial. Both Schick and Bowen have demonstrated what can be accomplished with rural and regional surveys.[2] Similar studies for areas of the trans-Missouri West would be a welcome addition not only for their descriptive value but also as a clue to American taste. Not until many such monographs are available can the definitive story of our stage be written.

Such a work, of course, would demand more biographical knowledge of actors, past and present, than now is available. Fayette L. Robinson, nineteenth-century manager of a troupe that toured the Middle West, needs further study; G. J. Adams and his company are little known; Kate Denin and Sallie St. Clair deserve investigation. The historian of the theater would profit by an interest in Robert Linn, Welsh Edwards, William Henderson. The Allen A. Brown collection in the Boston Public Library, the theater materials in Harvard University, the holdings of the New York Public Library and of the Library of Congress are full of suggestions.

[1] John H. Kendall, *The Golden Age of the New Orleans Theater* (Baton Rouge, 1952); G. C. D. Odell, *History of the New York Stage*, 15 vols. (New York, 1927-49).

[2] Joseph S. Schick, *The Early Theater in Eastern Iowa* (Chicago, 1939); Elbert R. Bowen, *Theatrical Entertainment in Rural Missouri before the Civil War* (Columbia, 1959).

The history of the legitimate theater cannot be considered complete until additional biographical research is devoted to playwrights, who squeeze social issues into three acts to reflect a people's foibles and virtues. A little more than a casual dipping into Adams's drama dictionary, Thomson's index, and Conway's syllabus would turn up ideas for projects.[3]

Rewards await researchers who continue to investigate popular images and stereotypes as they are depicted on the stage. There still is opportunity to probe deeply into the theater's portrayal of American types and characteristics, from the concept of Brother Jonathan, through that of the "sugar-daddy," to current representations of the Negro, the young egg-head, the girl who wants to get rich quick by striking oil. This materialistic, grasping woman, who appeared in the Broadway musical *Wildcat,* is a character of more substance than is usual in this type of production.[4]

To separate the stage from the motion picture and the motion picture from television is growing increasingly difficult. Actors may move from one medium to another with astonishing rapidity. Phil Silvers is an example. Beginning his career as a "breakdown singer" in a Brooklyn movie house, he took part in vaudeville, did burlesque skits, received a picture-making contract with Metro-Goldwyn-Mayer, was successful on TV, and, in 1960, appeared on Broadway as a star of *Do Re Me.* The cultural historian of tomorrow will, no doubt, feel that Silvers and others like him are as worthy of investigation as yesterday's

[3] William D. Adams, *Dictionary of the Drama: A Guide to the Plays, Playwrights, Players, and Playhouses of the United Kingdom and America, from the Earliest Times to the Present* (Philadelphia, 1904); Ruth G. Thomson, *Index to Full Length Plays, 1895 to 1925* (Boston, 1956); Blanch M. Baker, *Theatre and Allied Arts: A Guide to Books Dealing with the History, Criticism, and Technic of the Drama, and Theatre, and Allied Arts and Crafts* (New York, 1952); Harold Clurman, *The Fervent Years: The Story of the Group Theatre and the Thirties* (New York, 1957); John A. Conway, *Syllabus for History of the Theatre* (Seattle, 1951).

[4] See, for example, Howard Taubman, "Soft on Musicals," *The New York Times,* January 8, 1961, a comment on *Do Re Me:* "But it is Mr. Silvers' genius to have turned the glib, unscrupulous operator, a type we all have met, into a hilarious national symbol."

historians considered Alexander Drake, who played western circuits.

Today players, companies, broadcasting systems, and shows offer an almost unexplored field. Television soap opera, the western, the mystery—all these and more await the cultural historian. There will come a day, presumably, when the Dinah Shore show, Perry Mason, or "Have Gun Will Travel" may be assigned as topics for graduate students. Fortunately, guides now direct students to the nontechnical literature of radio and television, and the 1950s saw the publication of histories. Some accounts do not approach the subject as would a cultural historian, and this country has not kept pace with foreign nations in the publication of biographies, encyclopedias, and bibliographies.[5]

Although studies of steamboating on inland waterways are available, there is as yet no comprehensive, full-length monograph which unfolds the history of the traveling troupes which performed on showboats and on passenger vessels. Graham's *Showboats* restricts itself generally to the lower Mississippi.[6] Could not more studies be done for the upper river and for the

[5] Charles Reinert, *Kleines Filmlexikon: Kunst, Technik, Geschichte, Biographie, Schrifttum* (Einsiedeln-Zürich, 1946); Maud W. Miller, ed., *Winchester's Screen Encyclopedia* (London, 1948); University of Padua, Centro Cinematografico, *Bibliografia generale del cinema* (Rome, 1953); Library of Congress, Division of Bibliography, *Moving Pictures in the United States and Foreign Countries*, compiled by Anne L. Baden (Washington, 1940); Howard L. Walls, *Motion Picture Incunabula in the Library of Congress* (New York, 1944); Burton Paulu, comp., *A Radio and Television Bibliography: Books and Magazines on the Nontechnical Aspects of Broadcasting Published between January 1, 1949 and June 30, 1952* (Urbana, 1952); Marvin A. Asnes and others, *A History of the Television Industry, 1950-1960* (Boston, 1961); Orrin E. Dunlap, Jr., *Radio and Television Almanac: Men, Events, Inventions, and Dates That Made History from the Dawn of Electricity to Radio and Television* (New York, 1951); Abel Green and Joe Laurie, Jr., *Show Biz, from Vaude to Video* (New York, 1951); *International Motion Picture Almanac* (New York, 1947); D. E. Brown, "Radio and Television: An Annotated Bibliography," *Journalism Quarterly*, XXXIV (1957), 378-86.

[6] Philip Graham, *Showboats: The History of an American Institution* (Austin, 1951); R. L. Johnson, "Captain Menke's School for Actors: Showboat Goldenrod," *American Mercury*, LXXIX (1954), 109-10; A. Scheff, "Theatre on a Traveling Showboat," *Theatre Arts*, XXXVII (1953), 82-83.

Ohio and the Missouri? The day of the showboat is not entirely done; even now the one sponsored by the University of Minnesota plays to capacity houses night after night. Studies could be made of the wandering overland actors who, usually without props or scenery, invaded mining camps, cow towns, and railroad construction centers to speak their lines. Such itinerant performers are a colorful part of the theater record and deserve attention from the cultural historian.

The history of the corkfaces merits further exploration, although Wittke has already pictured the minstrel in delightful manner.[7] Whether this form of entertainment belongs to the theater or to music sometimes is debated, but my inclination is to place it in the general area of the playhouse. No one will deny, of course, that there is a difference between minstrel songs and the minstrel show. The point is that both can still be exploited profitably. It might be of worth, for example, to investigate the history of these shows in various communities, especially by searching local newspapers, and to prepare short sketches of famous end men. To the best of my knowledge no one has as yet gathered sufficient material on the publishing houses that specialized in printing instructions for minstrels, that frequently prepared handbooks of set jokes, and that occasionally issued pamphlets on prominent minstrel characters. Indeed, some enterprising person could make a contribution if he compiled a bibliography of minstrelsy. It would be valuable also to collect information on publishers who printed plays for the theater, a business which continues today. In addition to national publishers who issue working versions for actors there are smaller printers, such as The Torch Press in Cedar Rapids, Iowa.

Comprehensive histories of burlesque and vaudeville are yet to come. Only a slight excursion into these areas demonstrates that diligent research would turn up more information than is

---

[7] Carl Wittke, *Tambo and Bones: A History of the American Minstrel Stage* (Durham, 1930).

now at hand. On this side of the Atlantic what later was called burlesque originally began in waterfront dives frequented mostly by sailors. By the early decades of the nineteenth century, places of amusement not infrequently featured gyrations now associated with fan dancers and strip-tease artists. The middle 1840s saw an increase in this type of entertainment. After the Civil War burlesque began to sweep across the nation. This form of entertainment, here so briefly sketched, includes gaps to be filled and chapters to be written. We need, for example, histories of famous theaters that featured it, such as the Star and Garter in Chicago. We need to distinguish between "low" and "high" burlesque, to investigate the introduction of popular ditties into their programs, to place the entire story in its social setting. Certainly it is as worthy of study as the melodrama.

The narrative of vaudeville, a type of entertainment which developed in part from burlesque, awaits further exploration. Coming into its own after the Civil War, vaudeville probably reached its peak between the first World War and the early 1930s; but the USO shows, in a sense, continued the tradition. Although it did not always offer family-type entertainment, vaudeville generally was inoffensive, relying, at least in the better houses, more upon skill than smut—the skill of the magician and of the sleight-of-hand manipulator, of the comedian, of the singers of current tunes, of the men and women capable of producing a creditable farce that ran for fifteen minutes. The general history is known, but, here again, much has been lost and new material awaits the researcher. How did the typical vaudeville program develop? What were the major booking agencies and who were their managers? Who were the really talented ventriloquists, the jugglers, the so-called Irish and German humorists? What documentary sources are available? Where are they? How and why did vaudeville and burlesque fill a social and cultural need? Is it true that they developed because of the rise of laboring classes—workers unable to appreciate or enjoy more sophisticated entertainment? Was vaudeville the result of the leveling down of a democratic society? Sobel does not answer such questions in his book on burlesque and Gilbert does not do it for vaudeville.[8]

As much, if not more, needs to be done with the history of music. The same condition holds as for the theater: the evident has been investigated, the less obvious has been slighted or overlooked. And frequently it is the less patent that, when properly comprehended, radically alters generalized conclusions. What, then, might still be profitably researched?

Although the American Recording Project Committee of the Music Library Association has in progress a cooperatively written history of American music under the chairmanship of Irving Lowens, this work cannot possibly be definitive until, for example, the story of the traveling troupes of nineteenth-century singers has been exploited further. My tale of the famous Hutchinson Family from the Old Granite State is only the slightest footnote for a volume which should demonstrate the role that such songsters played, and should set forth the complete narrative of groups that marched, with voices triumphant, the length and breadth of the nation.[9] Troupes whose history awaits further attention include the Alleghanians, the Baker Vocalists, the Swiss Bell Ringers, the Spencer Family, Father Kemp's Old Folks Choir, the Continentals, the Bliss Family, the Mountain Vocalists, and others.

Perhaps street music, from the captivating cries of South Carolina vendors, through the vocalizing of chimney sweeps and even carpenters and handymen, to the German bands of a later day, deserves additional research. A New York editor in 1840 wrote: "There is a Swiss emigrant, with his whole family,

[8] Bernard Sobel, *Burleycue* (New York, 1931); Douglas Gilbert, *American Vaudeville* (New York, 1940); see also, Rowland Barber, *The Night They Raided Minsky's: A Fanciful Expedition to the Lost Atlantis of Show Business* (New York, 1960); we have for the United States no such volume as Victor C. Clinton-Baddeley, *The Burlesque Tradition in the English Theatre after 1660* (London, 1952).

[9] Philip D. Jordan, *Singin' Yankees* (Minneapolis, 1946).

including a little dog and a monkey, before our door, tuning their pipes and accompanying themselves on the tambourine and the triangle." Later the *New York Mirror* said: "The highways and by-ways, the dark alley and the broad thoroughfare of business—of fashion and of pleasure, have become the very opera-boxes of the city—the very paving-stones cry out."[10]

Curiously enough, more investigation should be devoted to the song entertainment provided on canal and river boats. It is known, of course, that theater boats, such as Chapman's Floating Theater, regularly cruised the Ohio and Mississippi rivers during the middle decades of the nineteenth century, but little information is available concerning the musical diversion contracted for by captains of passenger boats. Thomas L. Nichols, an American physician, pictured aspects of river entertainment vividly: "America can boast of some novelties in the way of amusement never seen in Europe—floating theatres and circuses, propelled by steam, going from town to town on the great western rivers, and carrying not only stage, auditorium, scenery, &c., but lodging and accommodations for the company, and, in the case of circuses, stabling and forage for the horses. . . . On the appointed day the floating theater comes in sight, flags flying, band playing, or a steam-organ filling the whole region with its obstreperous harmonies."[11]

Now and again the researcher picks up a tantalizing hint, such as this item which appeared in a New Orleans newspaper back in 1837: "The Steamer John Linton has fine music. Those who are going to Red River are advised to travel on board of her."[12] River music seems to be a somewhat fresh subject and one that, if diligently pursued, might contribute not only to the general knowledge of American musical performances but would also add to our knowledge of the amusement of the people.

It would be worth while if more cultural historians interested

[10] *New York Mirror*, January 4, April 11, 1840.
[11] Thomas L. Nicholas, *Forty Years of American Life* (New York, 1937), 189.
[12] *New Orleans Picayune*, September 19, 1837.

themselves in songs and ballads. A model is at hand in Blegen and Ruud's collection of Norwegian emigrant songs.[13] The same thing should be done for other peoples—the French, the Germans, the Swedes, the Italians, and now, the men and women who are arriving from Puerto Rico.

The laborer in the field of musical history can almost always produce a biography. Of the significant nineteenth-century composers and performers, the lives of many remain to be written. There is, obviously, no longer need for a biography of Stephen Foster or Jenny Lind, but there is still opportunity to do research on the activities of other artists who enriched our national song. For example, it would be possible to write a scholarly study of Edwin P. Christy, king of the minstrel show, and his sons. Although the sketch of Christy in the *Dictionary of American Biography* states that his name "stands first in point of time, and at the head of his profession," the appended citations number only three—a newspaper obituary of 1862, an English theatrical magazine of 1882, and a reference to a slight, and not particularly rewarding, account in *Harper's Magazine* for 1889. Not even Spaeth does Christy justice.[14]

The history of music publishers invites further study. True, the names of both publishers and their houses are general knowledge, but in some instances not much detail is available about either. A careful research job on the firm of Balmer and Weber of St. Louis would add to our store of knowledge. It would be well to learn more about Boston's Oliver Ditson and New York's Firth, Hall, and Pond. What about the Philadelphia and Cincinnati publishers and those of Minneapolis and San Francisco? Accounts of important musical periodicals of the nineteenth century, such as *Dwight's Journal of Music*, would be desirable.

Another diversion worth studying is the museum. From the phrenological halls of yesteryear to contemporary galleries of

[13] Theodore C. Blegen and Martin B. Ruud, *Norwegian Emigrant Songs and Ballads* (Minneapolis, 1936).
[14] Sigmund Spaeth, *History of Popular Music in America* (New York, 1948).

modern art there is abundant opportunity for the cultural researcher. A history of expositions of science, industry, and technology, and one of reconstruction projects, such as the one at Williamsburg, would be helpful. Open-air museums, like the Norwegian-American Historical Museum at Decorah, Iowa, offer attractive possibilities for research.[15]

Neither the circus nor the Wild West show has been interpreted fully, although considerable attention has been given each. Surprisingly enough, private collectors hold considerable source material, and these records must be located and used. Devotees of the big top know a new reference work, which describes holdings in the British Museum, the Library of Congress, the Bibliothèque Nationale.[16] The circus is not dead in the United States. When the Ringling Brothers and Barnum and Bailey Circus opened its new winter home in Venice, Florida, more than 10,000 persons, double the town's population, turned out in welcome. Shrine circuses delight children of the nation, and smaller shows prosper. As yet the story of the Shrine performances is untold as is the history of the Polack Brothers Circus.

Historians could use a trustworthy narrative which explains the place that card playing and gambling have in American life. A comprehensive history of games of chance could shed light on the national character and chart the development of an activity which has fascinated many, from colonial days to the time when the twinkling lights of Las Vegas began to

[15] Tora Bohn, "A Quest for Norwegian Folk Art in America," *Norwegian American Studies and Records*, XIX (1956), 116-41.

[16] Raymond T. Stott, *Circus and Allied Arts: A World Bibliography, 1500-1957*, 2 vols. (Derby, England, 1958-60), a third volume is in progress; see also, G. L. Chindahl, *A History of the Circus in America* (Caldwell, Idaho, 1959); John Durant, *Pictorial History of the American Circus* (New York, 1957); Marian Murray, *Circus! From Rome to Ringling* (New York, 1956); Henry Ringling North, *The Circus Kings: Our Ringling Family Story* (Garden City, 1960); Irving Wallace, *The Fabulous Showman: Life and Times of P. T. Barnum* (New York, 1959). The United States, however, lacks such works as: Alessandro Cervellati, *Bologna al Microscopio: Feste Spettacoli Divertimenti*, 3 vols. (Bologna, 1950); Raul H. Castagnino, *El Circo Criollo: Datas y Documentos Para su Historia, 1597-1924* (Buenos Aires, 1953).

beckon. Poker, monte, faro, roulette, whist, black jack—all these and others should be included. Wagers and bets are of interest. Benton, in a little book of 1893, wrote that frequently a can of peaches was a favorite stake in poker. Sol Smith, the actor, wrote of the game. Travelers have left innumerable descriptions of gamblers, betting houses, and customers. In a Sacramento saloon, wrote an observor in 1853, there were "tables for the A. B. C. game, and by them men rattling the 'bones,' the vulgar for dice; tables for roulette, and the attendants were shouting: 'red wins,' 'black takes it,' 'now's your time,' and so on; tables covered with blue or green cloth, with piles of silver and gold on them; at one, a man with French cards, taking people 'by the door;' at another, a man with American cards, inviting bets by 'spread outs,' . . . and at others men playing games that outsiders knew nothing of." Lillard's collection of poker stories is a mine of information. Thirty years have elapsed since the publication of an adequate history of playing cards, and, to the best of my knowledge, no bibliography of gambling ever has been compiled.[17]

The history of group sports now receives more attention than formerly, but still remains a challenge to those who wish to investigate the American emphasis upon athletics. First to be suggested are full-length studies of basketball, football, baseball. Seymour's recent work on the early years of baseball could serve as a pattern. Similiar monographs on secondary sports, such as wrestling and prize fighting, could be under-

[17] J. A. Benton, *The California Pilgrim* (Sacramento, 1893), 178, 218; J. D. Borthwick, *The Gold Hunters* (New York, 1922), ed. by Horace Kephardt; Walter Colton, *Three Years in California* (New York, 1855); William H. Milburn, *Ten Years of Preacher-Life* (New York, 1859); Sol Smith, *Theatrical Apprenticeship* (Philadelphia, 1846), 146-52; John F. B. Lillard, *Poker Stories 1845-1895* (New York, 1896); Catherine P. Hargrave, *History of Playing Cards and a Bibliography of Cards and Gaming* (Boston, 1930); Herbert L. Marx, ed., *Gambling in America* (New York, 1952); Katharine Best and Katharine Hillyer, *Las Vegas: Playtown U. S. A.* (New York, 1955); J. S. Ezell, *Fortune's Merry Wheel: the Lottery in America* (Cambridge, 1960); Foster R. Dulles, *America Learns to Play: A History of Popular Recreation, 1607-1940* (New York, 1952); Morris Ploscowe et al, "Gambling," *Annals of the American Academy of Political and Social Science*, CCLXIX (May, 1950), the entire issue.

taken.[18] Croquet, volleyball, and archery offer possibilities in relatively unworked fields.[19] When all this is accomplished, some enterprising person should bring together a history of all these activities, paying particular attention to their place in the nation's cultural pattern. There is a difference, in my mind, between the history of games and a history of the role of such games in mores and folkways.

The same approach could well be used for such sports as fishing, hunting, horse racing, and others. As early as the 1820s, the *American Turf Register and Sporting Magazine* was entertaining readers with accounts of trout fishing in Vermont and deer hunting in Virginia. As the frontier edged westward, so did the locale of such sporting tales. By the mid-1840s, out-of-door adventure literature was plentiful, appearing both in books and in periodicals such as *Porter's Spirit of the Times* and its counterpart on the west coast, the *California Spirit of the Times*, which merged with the *Fireman's Journal*. Higginson's adequate bibliography of British and American sports writers and Henderson's check list of early American sporting books offer assistance to research in these fields.[20]

---

[18] Harold Seymour, *Baseball: The Early Years* (New York, 1960); Lee Allen, *100 Years of Baseball, the Intimate and Dramatic Story of Modern Baseball from the Game's Beginnings up to the Present Day* (New York, 1950); Arthur Daley, *Times at Bat: A Half Century of Baseball* (New York, 1950); Allen Danzig, *History of American Football: Its Great Teams, Players, and Coaches* (Englewood Cliffs, 1956); Alexander M. Weyand, *Saga of American Football* (New York, 1955); Frank J. Basloe, *I Grew Up with Basketball: Twenty Years with Cage Greats of Yesterday* (New York, 1952); Guy Le Bow, *The Wrestling Scene* (New York, 1950); C. M. Wilson, *Magnificent Scufflers* (Brattleboro, Vermont, 1959); Louis Golding, *The Bareknuckle Breed* (New York, 1954); Abbott J. Liebling, *The Sweet Science* (New York, 1956). An examination of these titles demonstrates how much remains to be done.

[19] Paul Brown, *Croquet* (Princeton, 1957); the volleyball literature consists mostly of handbooks; Clement C. Parker, *Compendium of Works on Archery* (Philadelphia, 1950); Edmund Burke, *History of Archery* (New York, 1957) is, like so many others, a history of the sport, but fails to treat it as popular entertainment.

[20] A. Henry Higginson, *British and American Sporting Authors, Their Writings and Biographies* (Berryville, Virginia, 1949); Robert W. Henderson, *Early American Sport: A Check-list of Books by American and Foreign Authors Published in America prior to 1860, Including Sporting Songs* (New York, 1953).

It might be equally valuable to examine the history of the sporting magazine of both past and present. This is probably no task for the researcher in journalism, for he might produce a volume reciting only editorial policies, changes of editors, descriptions of formats. This job belongs to the cultural historian who, by the very nature of his training, would go beyond the technical and place the sporting press in its cultural framework. *The Horseman, Burton's Gentleman's Magazine, Sports of the Times, Field and Stream,* for example, could all be tilled with profit.

It is surprising that no historian has considered it worth while to pen a social and cultural history of the role of the rifle and the handgun. Of course, there are now in print histories of specific weapons—the Winchester, the Kentucky rifle, the Colt revolver.[21] Such studies frequently emphasize bore and calibre, model and size, weight and length. Of considerable interest to the gunsmith and to mechanically minded sportsmen, they lack appeal for the cultural historian. I look for a volume that pictures the gun in use—in the subjugation of the country, in hunting. Mary W. Berthel has come close to such an approach in an account of hunting in Minnesota, but there is no book which treats the subject in this manner.[22]

Some years ago, thinking about old-time Fourth-of-July celebrations, with the booming of giant firecrackers, the multihued glory of Roman candles, the flimsy paper balloons, I wondered why there should not be a history of fireworks. They amused folk during the Ming Dynasty, pleased residents of Nürnberg in 1650, and have delighted young and old in practically every

[21] Harold F. Williamson, *Winchester: The Gun That Won the West* (Washington, D. C., 1952); John G. W. Dillon, *The Kentucky Rifle* (Washington, D. C., 1924); William B. Edwards, *The Story of Colt's Revolver* (Harrisburg, 1953); Martin Rywell, *Samuel Colt, a Man and an Epoch* (Harriman, Tennessee, 1953); the best bibliographical guide is Raymond L. J. Riling, *Guns and Shooting: A Selected Chronological Bibliography* (New York, 1951), which does refer to the use of firearms in sport; see also, Carl P. Russell, *Guns on the Early Frontiers* (Berkeley, 1951); Arthur M. Carey, *American Firearms Makers* (New York, 1953).

[22] Mary W. Berthel, "Hunting in Minnesota in the Seventies," *Minnesota History,* XVI (1935), 259-71.

nation. I decided to see what sort of bibliography might be prepared. The result was an annotated list of some two thousand items, for the period 1776 to 1900. References were drawn from books, diaries, journals, periodicals, histories of the stage, city annals, newspapers. They were arranged under various categories: manufacturers and their biographies; uses on the stage, in magic, on holidays, in political demonstrations, for national celebrations, and military pyrotechny; simple and compound fireworks; related accidents; advertising; legislation; tales and yarns.

The bibliography indicated gaps to be filled. A study could be made, for example, of the use of fireworks in the major entertainment palaces of cities—New York's Niblo Gardens, Vauxille Garden, Dempsey's Long Room, Castle Garden; of displays used on holidays and for celebrations of special events; of the relationship between fireworks and magic; of the little-known history of manufacturing firms. The last mentioned would include Holden and Cutter and C. E. Masten of Boston; Detwiller and Street, Unexcelled Fireworks Company, Charles H. Koster, Pain's Pyro-Spectacle Company of New York; and L. Soards and Company and McGraw, Morris, and Tchoupitoulas of New Orleans.[23]

The United States could use a cultural history of this popular amusement. Such a book must not be a history of fireworks, as is Brock's volume, which excludes the United States, but a narrative of the people's use and enjoyment of pyrotechnics.[24] It must incorporate the spirit of scenes such as this: "A number of small boys were engaged yesterday afternoon in Chartres street, in the appropriate amusement of the day—firing crackers. Opposite to them were a dozen or so of children . . . clustered around a very large toy shop window. The fire cracker urchins presently placed a small rocket in a crack in the gutter curb

[23] *Boston Daily Advertiser,* July 4, 1815; *New Orleans Daily Picayune,* December 25, 1855; for magic and tales, see George Arnold, *The Magician's Own Book* (New York, 1857); "Fireworks at Home and Abroad," *Cornhill Magazine,* LII (1885), 290-98.
[24] Alan St. H. Brock, *A History of Fireworks* (London, 1949).

stone, lit a match, and silently awaited events. . . . The rocket exploded just as we werê passing. . . . We heard the sound, barely caught a glimpse of the course of the missle, so swiftly did it fly—a tall gentleman opposite and in the crowd around the toy shop window made a very sudden dodge, and the crash of glass immediately following, announced a disaster to some one's panes of glass. . . . The toy shop window was damaged 'purty considerable'; the boys shouted; the neighbors stared; the shop-keeper came out in a fury in an old morning gown; and we vanished. . . . Moral: rocket and boys are dangerous products: avoid them—in the street."[25]

It is simplicity itself to suggest areas to be investigated and specific tasks to be undertaken. It is far more difficult to initiate and bring projects to completion. The researcher all too frequently is hung upon three diabolically sharp thorns— lack of time, lack of financial support, lack of bibliographical aid. My assignment would be incomplete without a comment upon the imperative need for better bibliographic organization. The sad truth is that contemporary problems of bibliographic techniques may well impede, if not halt, many of the stimulating suggestions made during this conference. Indeed, so concerned am I, that I wish a group might meet to discuss reforms in bibliographic procedure and organization.

In the first place, the scholar desperately needs more indexes to more newspapers, both past and present. It is almost literally true that the newspaper, an indispensable source, with few exceptions is unindexed. Most of the recommendations for research projects that have been made here depend upon an examination of newspapers. Perhaps machine searching is the answer. Perhaps history departments, in cooperation with library schools, should train more bibliographers. We need also abstracts and summaries of the contents of the nation's press. The *Annals of Cleveland*, efficient, useful, practical, is an example. Finally, it is desirable that such titles as the American Historical Association's *Writings on American His-*

[25] *New Orleans Daily Picayune*, December 26, 1851.

tory and Winchell's *Guide to Reference Books* be put into print more regularly and more promptly than they now are. The last volume of the former covers 1953, and the last supplement to the latter lists publications for 1956-1958.

Books, periodicals, newspapers comprise an almost unmanageable area. The recovery of information grows increasingly difficult. It will continue to be so until systematic effort, sponsored by generous grants from both private and federal funds, brings sources under bibliographic control. It is recommended that the "historical societies of this country explore the possibility of long-term federal grants to assure prompt publication of projects already under way, to expand existing publication programs, to increase grants generally and post-doctoral fellowships in particular, to underwrite the purchase of scanning machines, to assist in the training of persons to operate them, to establish regional bibliographic research centers."[26]

Some such imaginative and practical program is the only sure way to implement and bring into print a broad program of research such as has been suggested by those of us here, who are concerned with opportunities for research in American cultural history.

[26] Philip D. Jordan, "The Historian and the Contemporary Problem of Bibliographic Techniques," *American Documentation,* X (1959), 267-69; also, Jordan, "Whose Mirror is a Pitiful Affair: Comments on Social and Cultural History," *The Present World of History,* James H. Rodabaugh, ed. (Madison, 1959), 108-15.

THE CONTRIBUTORS

THEODORE C. BLEGEN, dean emeritus of the Graduate School in the University of Minnesota, has been the editor in chief of the Norwegian-American Historical Association since its founding in 1925. During World War II, he served as director of the National Historical Service, which prepared materials for the Army's G. I. Roundtable. Dean Blegen is the author or editor of more than twenty books, among them *Building Minnesota; Grass Roots History; The Land Lies Open; Norwegian Migration to America; Lincoln's Imagery;* and *Land of their Choice.*

LESTER J. CAPPON is director of the Institute of Early American History and Culture, Williamsburg, Virginia, and archival consultant of Colonial Williamsburg. Before joining the Institute, he was archivist and professor of history in the University of Virginia. His publications include *Bibliography of Virginia History since 1865; Virginia Newspapers, 1821-1935; Iron Works at Tuball . . . of Alexander Spotswood;* and *The Adams-Jefferson Letters.*

THOMAS D. CLARK joined the faculty of the University of Kentucky in 1931. Now chairman of the department of history, he has long been actively engaged in research and writing on southern history, the frontier movement, and the history of Kentucky. He is the author of *Rampaging Frontier; History of Kentucky; Pills, Petticoats, and Plows; Southern Country Editor;* and *Frontier America;* and editor of the six-volume collection, *Travels in the South.*

RICHARD M. DORSON, editor of the Journal of American Folk-lore, is professor of history and folklore and chairman of the folklore program at Indiana University. His books include *Jonathan Draws the Long Bow; Bloodstoppers and Bear-walkers; Negro Folktales in Michigan;* and *American Folklore.*

JOSEPH EWAN, since 1947 professor of botany at Tulane University, is the author of numerous studies in the history of natural sciences, including *Rocky Mountain Naturalists.* In 1956 he was an official delegate of the French government to a Paris conference on the history of Franco-American botany. Before joining the faculty at Tulane, he was associated with the U. S. Department of Agriculture Bureau of Plant Industry, the Smithsonian Institution, the Foreign Economic Administration, and the University of Colorado. His latest book is *John Banister and His Natural History of Virginia, 1692.*

JOHN T. FLANAGAN has been professor of English in the University of Illinois since 1949. His interest in American folklore and in the literature and culture of the Middle West has resulted in publications which include *James Hall; America Is West; The American Way;* and (with A. P. Hudson) *Folklore in American Literature.*

PHILIP D. JORDAN, professor of history in the University of Minnesota, is the author of *William Salter: Western Torch-bearer; Ohio Comes of Age: 1873-1900; Singin' Yankees; The National Road; The People's Health; Uncle Sam of America; Fiddlefoot Jones of the North Woods; Songs of Yesterday* (with L. Kessler); and *With Various Voices* (with T. C. Blegen). Mr. Jordan is a director of the Folk Arts Foundation of America and editor of the Mississippi Valley Press.

DAVID KASER, author of *Messrs. Carey & Lea of Philadelphia,* has also contributed articles on American publishing history to a number of scholarly periodicals. He is now director of the

Joint University Libraries, Nashville, and professor of library science in Vanderbilt University, Peabody College, and Scarritt College.

JOHN FRANCIS McDERMOTT has been a member of the faculty of Washington University, St. Louis, since 1924. He has written or edited sixteen books in the fields of French-American relations, social and cultural history of the Mississippi Valley, and the literature of travel. His publications include *Private Libraries in Creole Saint Louis; A Glossary of Mississippi Valley French, 1673-1850; The Lost Panoramas of the Mississippi;* and *George Caleb Bingham, River Portraitist.*

DAVID MEAD, now chairman of the department of English in Michigan State University, joined the Michigan State staff in 1948. He served from 1955 to 1957 as chief of the Michigan State Advisory Group at the University of the Ryukyus, Okinawa, where he developed an English language program. He is the author of *Yankee Eloquence in the Middle West,* and at present he is writing a history of the public lecture in America.

HOWARD H. PECKHAM, author of *Pontiac and the Indian Uprising, Captured by Indians,* and *The War for Independence,* is director of the William L. Clements Library at the University of Michigan. A former newspaperman, he has served as curator of manuscripts at the Clements Library, as director of the Indiana Historical Bureau, and as associate editor of *American Heritage.*

EDGAR P. RICHARDSON is the author of four books on art history, of which the most recent is *Painting in America.* One of his major interests has been the study of American art as one of the great national schools within the framework of western art. He is director of the Detroit Institute of Arts and of the Archives of American Art and editor of *The Art Quarterly.*

INDEX

Abbott, John, 85
Abel, Annie Heloise, 22
Adair, James, 51n
Adam, T. R., 160
Adamic, Louis, 76
Adams, Evelyn C., 42n
Adams, G. J., 176
Adams, Herbert Baxter, 5
Adams, William D., 177
Adams, William E., 56n
Ade, George, 129
Agassiz, Louis, 165
Ager, Waldemar, 136
Aimard, Gustave, 29
Alden, J. E., 153
Alden, John R., 38n
Alexander, Edward P., 160
Alleghanians, the, 181
Allen, Lee, 186n
American Quarterly, 12
Ander, O. F., 79
Anderson, Sherwood, 129, 137
Andrews, Charles N.: important studies of colonial history, 6-7, 8, 10
Andrews, Sidney, 58n
Angle, Paul, 161
Archives of American Art, 173
Arese, Count Francesco, 55n
Arts, visual: dearth of studies on, 168-70; scholarship on, 169-72 *passim;* value of local material in research, 170; regional collections in museums, 171-72
——, suggested research on: biographies of artists, 169-70; history of arts and crafts of cities, 170; effect of technology on domestic arts, 170-71; regional material, 171-72; iconography of cities and regions, 172;

Arts, visual (*continued*):
history of art institutions, 172-73; marketing and collecting, 173; history of taste, 173-74
Asbury, Herbert, 19
Ashton, Joseph N., 159n
Asnes, Marvin A., 178n
Athearn, Robert, 58n
Atwater, Caleb, 127
Auer, J. Jeffery, 156n, **162**
Aurner, C. R., 157

Babcock, C. Merton, 117n
Bachman, John, 101n
Baden, Anne L., 178n
Badins (Badinsse), Louis, 24-25
Badollet, Jean, 21
Bailey, Lydia, 153
Bailyn, Bernard, 6n, 14
Baker, Blanch M., 177n
Baker Vocalists, 181
Baldwin, Alice N., 163
Balmer and Weber (publishers), 183
Balys, Jonas, 118
Bancroft, George, 2, 3
Banér, Skulda, 134
Banister, John: mentioned, 83; quoted, 92-93
Barbé-Marbois, François Marquis de, 51n
Barnard, Henry, 167
Barry, Colman J., 74, 75n
Barry, Phillips, 105, 107
Barton, Benjamin Smith: quoted, 84-85
Bartram, John, 47n, 51n
Bartram, William, 84
Basloe, Frank J., 186n
Bassett, Fletcher S., 105

DUE